40/40

40 DAYS TO RENEW YOUR MIND, TRANSFORM YOUR LIFE

PHIL GREEN

'...BE CHANGED ... BY A NEW WAY OF THINKING.'
Romans 12:2

Copyright © 2012 Scripture Union
First published 2012
ISBN 978 1 84427 727 8

Scripture Union
207–209 Queensway, Bletchley, Milton Keynes, MK2 2EB
Email: info@scriptureunion.org.uk
Website: www.scriptureunion.org.uk

Scripture quotations taken from THE HOLY BIBLE, NEW INTERNATIONAL VERSION
(Anglicised edition) Copyright © 1979, 1984, 2011 by Biblica (formerly International
Bible Society). Used by permission of Hodder & Stoughton Publishers, an Hachette
UK company. All rights reserved.

The Bible verse on the cover is from The New Century Version, © 1993 Thomas Nelso

Designed by Heather Knight
Printed by Nutech Print Services, India
Cover image: ©Istockphoto.com/Chris Schmidt

Scripture Union is an international Christian charity working with churches in
more than 130 countries.

Thank you for purchasing this book. Any profits from this book support SU in Englan
and Wales to bring the good news of Jesus Christ to children, young people and
families and to enable them to meet God through the Bible and prayer.

Find out more about our work and how you can get involved at:
www.scriptureunion.org.uk (England and Wales)
www.suscotland.org.uk (Scotland)
www.suni.org (Northern Ireland)
www.scriptureunion.org (USA)
www.su.org.au (Australia)

CONTENTS

ABOUT THE AUTHOR

Phil Green wrote 40/40 while living in rural Uganda, where he was training church leaders, leading project management courses, and setting up a charity. He is now back in the UK and working for the Evangelical Alliance. He is passionate about helping people connect faith to every area of their life.

He is married to Hannah, and enjoys watching films and eating good food in rural pubs. Previously he has authored a number of youth resources, including SUbstance, for Scripture Union.

INTRODUCTION

Whatever is noble, whatever is right, whatever is pure, whatever is lovely, whatever is admirable – if anything is excellent or praiseworthy – think about such things.'
Philippians 4:8

My mind never seems to rest. More often than not it feels like there is a hamster on a wheel in my head! I've spoken to several people about this, and it appears I'm not the only one. I suspect you, like me, have a highly active mind.

At school, I seem to remember being taught that the mind was the control centre for the body. It's no surprise that I find that what's going on in my mind not only affects my entire body, it has a big influence over my entire life.

Therefore, the confession I'm about to make presents me with a problem. Too often, the thoughts that race around my mind are not particularly healthy. And, this bad diet of thoughts must surely have a negative impact on my life, and, by association, the lives of those around me.

Is what I'm saying resonating with you? Consider for a moment what you think about when your mind has the opportunity to think about whatever it likes. For example, what do you think about as you lie in bed?

- Are your thoughts anxious ones? Are you constantly worrying about this, that or the other? Perhaps your thoughts stem from the insecurities you have about yourself.

- Are your thoughts angry ones? Is your mind a bitter place, full of resentment? Maybe you often find your mind plotting the downfall of someone who is making your life difficult.

- Are your thoughts happy ones? Perhaps you are fortunate and find yourself, on the whole, thinking about loved ones, happy memories and anticipation of future special moments with those you care about the most.

- Are your thoughts sexual ones? Do you find yourself fantasising about people you'd like to have a romantic encounter with? Perhaps your mind is well practised at imagining having sex with people that you're not married to.

- Are your thoughts ambitious ones? Maybe you find yourself dreaming of having lots of money, or getting your ideal job, or changing the world. Perhaps you imagine what you'd do if you were elected Prime Minister.

- Or perhaps you think about something else entirely. Whatever you think about, here's the key question: are they healthy thoughts that are making you godlier, or are they thoughts that are rotting your mind?

This is what the apostle Paul says in his letter to the church at Philippi:

Finally, brothers, whatever is true, whatever is noble, whatever is right, whatever is pure, whatever is lovely, whatever is admirable – if anything is excellent or praiseworthy – think about such things. Philippians 4:8

I have to say that, all too often, my thoughts are not true, noble, right, pure, lovely or admirable. Too many of my thoughts are not healthy and they're not making me godlier. Instead, they are rotting my mind.

The aim of the next 40 days is to develop a way of reading the Bible that makes your mind a healthier place. Reading the Bible should change your mind and transform your life. But does it? Too many of us just spend a few minutes reading the Bible each

day and tick it off our 'to-do list'. It might make us feel good –
knowing that we've 'done it' – and sometimes we might learn
something. However, does it really make a difference? This book
is about developing Bible reading habits that will change the
way you think, and as your mind becomes a healthier place, the
impact will be seen in your entire life.

INSTRUCTIONS

Do not conform to the pattern of this world, but be transformed by the renewing of your mind. Then you will be able to test and approve what God's will is – his good, pleasing and perfect will.
Romans 12:2

The aim of the next 40 days is to kick-start the process of renewing your mind. The method for doing this is not complicated; it's been about for millennia, and there's no brain surgery involved.

My experience has taught me that it's impossible to stop your mind thinking about something. The more you try and stop, the more you end up thinking about the thing you're trying to stop thinking about. Therefore, the next 40 days are not about thought-removal! Rather, they're about thinking about different things, so you forget to think about the unhealthy things.

Each morning and each evening read the suggested passage of Scripture. Read it through a few times and then think about it. By this I don't mean just think about it for a few minutes and then stop. Let it occupy your mind, let the thoughts move into your mind and put roots down. The word the Bible uses for this is meditation, and the psalmists talked about it quite a lot. We're encouraged to meditate on God's law both in the day and at night (Psalm 1:2), his precepts (instructions, guiding principles, Psalm 119:15) and his promises (Psalm 119:148).

However, this book is much more than a list of Bible passages for you to read. It aims to help you to think about the words you read, in order that these thoughts take root, so that you'll experience the renewal of your mind.

In the morning

As well as a passage to read, there is a brief commentary that provides context for the passage and will hopefully kick-start, and possibly guide, your thoughts. Make sure you reread the passage after you've read the commentary. My intention is that you spend the day thinking about God's words, not my words! The commentary is followed by a short prayer to invite God to become part of your thinking. Also, instead of thinking about the whole passage, you may like to focus your attention on just one phrase or idea from it.

We all have different routines in the morning; however, my advice would be to read the passage as early on in your day as possible. That might be before you get out of bed, while you eat breakfast or as you make your way to work. What's important is that you find a time that works for you.

Let me emphasise again that the aim of this is not just for you to think about the passage for a few minutes before getting on with the rest of the day. No! The aim is for the passage to dwell in your mind for the entire day.

'Oh, how I love your law! I meditate on it all day long.'
Psalm 119:97

Therefore, there are four ideas every morning to help you do this.

Firstly, there's a question for you to ponder. This will hopefully keep you thinking about the passage throughout the day.

Secondly, there's a conversation starter. Don't just think about the passage; stamp the passage onto your mind by talking about it. Sometimes you'll want to chat to a fellow Christ-follower, but more often than not the conversation starters will work with anyone you know. In fact sometimes they'll work best with a complete stranger!

These commandments that I give you today are to be on your hearts. Impress them on your children. Talk about them when you sit at home and when you walk along the road, when you lie down and when you get up.'
Deuteronomy 6:6,7

Thirdly, this passage in Deuteronomy goes onto say:

Tie them as symbols on your hands and bind them on your foreheads. Write them on the door-frames of your houses and on your gates. Deuteronomy 6:8

Therefore, there will be an idea that involves writing or drawing the passage, or representing it in a symbolic way. Some ideas will be more creative than others!

Fourthly, an action will be suggested, so that you're not just thinking about the passage, but it can be implemented practically in your life.

What's important to realise is that these four ideas are not four steps of a magic formula, that, if you do all of them, every day, will result in your mind being renewed. Rather, they are simply ideas to help you think about the passage and let it take root in your mind. Therefore, you don't have to religiously do all four ideas every day, just do whatever helps you.

The final piece of information to provide you with concerning the morning passages is that they work their way through the narrative of the Bible. The idea is that this will enable you to connect your story (life) to God's big story (human existence).

In the evening

Don't panic! When it comes to the evening passage there is not a short commentary to read or a series of activities to work through! I suggest you read the passage (a few times) once you're in bed and about to turn the lights off. Use the short prayer provided to direct your own prayers and then there is a question for you to ponder as you drift off to sleep.

Before you start...

...there are just a couple more things to say. There are some questions after every five days to help you think about what you're reading with others if you'd like to do that. There's also regular 'journal' space for you to write down your thoughts.

This book on its own is not meant to replace Bible study, family prayer times, small group activities or anything else that you're currently doing to help in your living a healthy Christ-centred life, but to be used alongside those things.

... be transformed by the renewing of your mind ...
Romans 12:2

in the beginning

In the beginning was the Word, and the Word was with God, and the Word was God. He was with God in the beginning. Through him all things were made; without him nothing was made that has been made. In him was life, and that life was the light of all mankind. The light shines in the darkness, but the darkness has not overcome it. John 1:1–5

I was once told that if you take 'Christ' out of the word Christian, you're left with 'Ian'. Now, I'm sure Ian is a lovely man, but, I doubt we should put our trust in him as our Saviour, and submit our lives to him as our Lord. We must never remove, or even diminish, the person of Christ from our Christianity. Neither, if we profess to be Christians, should we make Christ anything less than the centre of our lives.

Jesus Christ (aka 'the Word') is not just some wise, miracle-performing teacher who wowed the crowds, cared for the poor and annoyed a range of authority figures. John opens his Gospel with some information that, if true, should alter our understanding of the universe and change the direction of our lives. He is eternal. He is our Creator. He is God. He is the Light. And he wants to be the light of our lives.

All too many people reject Jesus, simply because they misunderstand him. Even many people who say they follow Jesus miss out on his light, because they too misunderstand him.

pray

Jesus… reveal to me today who you really are; help me to understand a little bit more about your character, your plans for the world and your plans for my life. I ask you at every opportunity to nudge me away from darkness and into your light. Amen.

ponder

What would be different if Jesus' light flooded into the dark areas of your life, your family, your church, your community, your nation, our world?

chat

Ask someone what they believe about Jesus. If that gets a conversation started, go on to explore whether they think his life bears any significance for us at the beginning of the twenty-first century.

write

Find a sticky label, or a strip of masking tape, and write either 'Jesus' or 'Jesus: the light of the world' on it. Then, attach it to a light switch that you frequently use.

action

Identify someone you know who is in a dark place at the moment. Do something today that will bring a little bit of light into their life. For example, send them an encouraging text, invite them out for a drink, surprise them with a chocolate bar, or give them a hug.

DAY 1: EVENING

This is the message we have heard from him and declare to you: God is light; in him there is no darkness at all. If we claim to have fellowship with him yet walk in the darkness, we lie and do not live out the truth. But if we walk in the light, as he is in the light, we have fellowship with one another, and the blood of Jesus, his Son, purifies us from all sin. 1 John 1:5–7

pray

Father God… I'm sorry for the times today that I have not walked in the light. I apologise for my dark words, deeds and thoughts. Forgive me, and as I sleep in physical darkness, may you bathe me in spiritual light. Tomorrow, guide me away from darkness and into the light. Amen.

ponder

What situations are you likely to find yourself in tomorrow that could easily result in you walking in darkness? How would walking in the light transform those situations?

the image of God

Then God said, 'Let us make mankind in our image, in our likeness, so that they may rule over the fish in the sea and the birds in the sky, over the livestock and all the wild animals, and over all the creatures that move along the ground.' So God created mankind in his own image, in the image of God he created them; male and female he created them. Genesis 1:26,27

The Babylonians described their kings as being 'the image of the gods'. As the image of the gods they were considered to be the gods' representatives here on earth. Following this logic, here is what the writer of Genesis is saying: 'The Babylonians think their kings are made in the image of the gods and represent the gods here on earth. But I tell you the truth; you are made in the image of the one true God. You are a representative of the Creator and Ruler of the universe.'

It's easy to feel inadequate! Science has revealed that the universe is massive and that this little planet we call home is really rather small. Population figures reveal that you are only one of 6.9 billion people. And then there are many 'voices' telling us that unless we wear the right clothes, have the latest gadgets and have a particular job we're inadequate. The feeling of inadequacy is sweeping through the world like a nasty disease.

The creation story should help destroy that feeling of inadequacy. God created you, in his image; his plan was for you to represent him on earth.

pray

Creator God… remove the feelings of inadequacy that I so often have and replace them with feelings of significance. Help me to grasp what it means to be made in your image, and equip me to represent you well today. Amen.

ponder

The role of a British Ambassador is to represent the interests of Great Britain in a foreign country. How can you best represent the interests of God today?

chat

Have a conversation with someone about why so many people today seem to have such low self-esteem. Why do they think this is the case? If appropriate, talk to them about how your belief in God as Creator transforms how you view your identity.

write

Write out today's passage on a sticky note and stick it to a mirror.

action

God put us in charge of life on his planet – we're meant to be taking care of it. However, we're frequently reminded that we're not doing a great job – our planet is suffering as a consequence of human actions. Spend a few minutes today thinking about how you could make a small lifestyle change to help care for the planet. If you're stuck for ideas, a few minutes looking online will point you in the right direction!

DAY 2: EVENING

For you created my inmost being; you knit me together in my mother's womb. I praise you because I am fearfully and wonderfully made; your works are wonderful, I know that full well. My frame was not hidden from you when I was made in the secret place, when I was woven together in the depths of the earth. Your eyes saw my unformed body.
Psalm 139:13–16a

pray
Father God… your creation is awesome. It's both beautiful and plentiful. I therefore find it staggering that you took so much care creating me and that you take such a close interest in my life. Help me focus less on created things, and instead focus more of my admiration on my Creator. Amen.

ponder
Depending on what state your body is in, it can sometimes be hard to consider it wonderful, or a reason to praise God. However, as you fall asleep tonight, think about some of the things you've been able to achieve and enjoy, because of the body God gave you. Take these thoughts, and turn them into praise.

DAY 3: MORNING

the pouncing beast

'If you do what is right, will you not be accepted? But if you do not do what is right, sin is crouching at your door; it desires to have you, but you must rule over it.' Genesis 4:7

The world God created was perfect, but it didn't stay perfect for long. Sin ruined it. Adam and Eve, followed by every person (apart from Jesus) to have walked on the earth since, disobeyed God. Genesis 3 tells the story of what went wrong – Adam and Eve's disobedience, their motivation, the consequences and God's response. However, this morning's verse is the first time the actual word 'sin' is found in the Bible. It provides an extremely poignant and accurate picture of what sin is like.

Sin likes to pounce on us; sometimes it takes us by surprise, but sadly it is often so obvious and familiar we barely notice it. Sin is quite like a snake – easy to pick up, difficult to put back down! As long as you're careful it is (apparently) relatively easy to pick up a snake. However, as snakes don't particularly like being handled, putting them back down can be tricky as they can be quite eager to strike. Once you start sinning, it's hard to stop. One lie leads to another. One lustful thought leads to another. Anger boils till it's uncontrollable.

If you don't learn how to control sin, it will control you.

pray
Lord God… I need your help. I've picked up sin. I keep trying to put it back down, but whenever I do, it pounces again. Help me put it down and give me the strength to not pick it up again. Amen.

ponder
What is crouching – metaphorically speaking – in the doorways of your life? (Don't just look at the obvious doorways; check the hidden ones as well.)

chat
Contact a trusted friend and tell them about what's crouching in the doorways of your life. Ask them to support you as you seek to master sin. Encourage them to pray for you and hold you accountable.

write
If you can find a soft-toy version of a pouncing animal (eg cat or tiger) place it safely by a doorway in your house, to act as a visual reminder that sin is waiting to pounce. Alternatively, you might like to draw a pouncing animal, write today's verse on it, and stick it on a door.

action
The chances are you already know one or two of the times you're likely to sin today. Be proactive! Before you get to that point in your day, plan what you're going to do differently so that you can do what is right rather than what is wrong. Control it; don't let it control you.

DAY 3: EVENING

Therefore, since we are surrounded by such a great cloud of witnesses, let us throw off everything that hinders and the sin that so easily entangles. And let us run with perseverance the race marked out for us, fixing our eyes on Jesus, the pioneer and perfecter of faith. For the joy that was set before him he endured the cross, scorning its shame, and sat down at the right hand of the throne of God.
Hebrews 12:1,2

pray
Loving God… today I have recognised some of the sin that so often entangles me. Sometimes, becoming untangled seems like such hard work I wonder if it's worth it. Help me to make the effort. I thank Jesus for enduring the cross in order for my sin to be dealt with. I want to fix my eyes on Jesus; I want to stop my eyes getting distracted by sin. Amen.

ponder
How would your relationships, your work, your bank account, your problems, your entire life be different if your eyes were first and foremost fixed on Jesus?

DAY 4: MORNING

be a blessing

'I will make you into a great nation and I will bless you; I will make your name great, and you will be a blessing. I will bless those who bless you, and whoever curses you I will curse; and all peoples on earth will be blessed through you.'
Genesis 12:2,3

After the wonderful opening scene of the Bible (Creation), the next few chapters pan out like a disaster movie. Sin rages out of control like wildfire. Then, in chapter 12 there's a fresh start. God approaches a man called Abram (later his name is changed to Abraham) and the story of God's people, the Israelites, begins.

God's people would become a great nation, God would reveal himself to them and they would be blessed. However, and this is really key, because more often than not the Israelites missed this salient point(!) God didn't bless them in order to have 'favourites' or create a more superior people group. No. No. No. He revealed himself to them, so they could reveal him to the whole world. He blessed them, so they could bless others. The culmination of the promise God made Abram was Jesus ('... all peoples on earth will be blessed through you').

It's easy to be critical of the Israelites, but first we should examine ourselves. God hasn't just revealed himself to you for your benefit, but also for the benefit of the people around you. If God has blessed you in any way, don't keep the blessings to yourself – share the love.

pray

God Almighty… thank you for not giving up on the human race, despite our disobedience. Thank you for revealing yourself to us and seeking us out to have a relationship with you. You've given me so much – spiritually and physically. Help me not to be selfish with this, but to be a blessing to others. Amen.

ponder

How has God blessed you and how can you make sure that instead of keeping these blessings to yourself you share them with others?

chat

Speak to a friend about whether we really appreciate what we have. Do we take it all for granted? Do we consider it a right? How could we better appreciate what we have? How can we use what we have more wisely? (Don't limit the conversation to material possessions.)

write

Write (or type) the words 'Blessed to be a blessing' somewhere prominent. For example, you could set it as the welcome message on your mobile phone or the screensaver on your computer.

action

Bless someone today in a way that stems from how you've been blessed. For example, if you have a comfortable home, invite people around for a meal. If you can afford to buy a cup of coffee everyday from Starbucks, buy a homeless person a cup of coffee. If your gifting is poetry, write someone a poem.

And by faith even Sarah, who was past childbearing age, was enabled to bear children because she considered him faithful who had made the promise. And so from this one man, and he as good as dead, came descendants as numerous as the stars in the sky and as countless as the sand on the seashore. All these people were still living by faith when they died. They did not receive the things promised; they only saw them and welcomed them from a distance, admitting that they were foreigners and strangers on earth. Hebrews 11:11–13

pray

God in heaven… sometimes I doubt the promises I read in the Bible. Sometimes I doubt you have things under control. Sometimes I question your plans. Remind me that the Scriptures are bursting at the seams with stories of your faithfulness. I should put my trust in you, because you are faithful. Amen.

ponder
What has happened in your life to give you reason to have faith in God?

great plans, unusual methods

But Joseph said to them, 'Don't be afraid. Am I in the place of God? You intended to harm me, but God intended it for good to accomplish what is now being done, the saving of many lives. So then, don't be afraid. I will provide for you and your children.' And he reassured them and spoke kindly to them. Genesis 50:19–21

The story of Joseph (Abraham's great-grandson) is one of the most well known in the Bible (Genesis 37 – 50). That's no surprise; it's a story that resonates with many of us.

Joseph aspired to greatness, but his journey to great things was not a direct one! His brothers wanted to kill him, but settled with selling him into slavery instead. He became a well-respected slave in Egypt, but then was unfairly accused of rape and found himself in prison. But he ended up being appointed Pharaoh's right-hand man and his successful management meant that Egypt avoided a famine. When Abraham's descendants (Joseph's brothers) realised there was food in Egypt they made the journey and found themselves begging their long-lost brother for food. It's a story full of 'buts'.

God had great plans for Joseph's life: plans that resulted in many people, including God's people the Israelites, not starving to death! But, the way God carried out his plans was not straightforward. Through Joseph's experience we learn important lessons for life.
• No matter what's going on, God is with us.
• God uses our experiences to shape us.
• God is the master of making good from bad.
• God's plans will prevail.

pray

Ruler of the universe… help me cling to the knowledge of your great plans. Help me accept that your plans are better than my plans. Help me trust you when everything around me is going wrong. Help me know and acknowledge your presence in the good times and the bad. Amen.

ponder

What bad situations and seemingly dead ends has God used in your life to get you to where he wants you?

chat

Talk with a friend or family member about the ups and downs of their life and whether any good came out of the bad situations they've experienced. If appropriate, share some of your experiences and share how your trust in God affects your perspective.

write

Draw a quick picture, or jot down a few words, that represent an unpleasant situation you're currently experiencing. Next to the picture or words, or even over the top, write the words 'God is the master of making good from bad.'

action

On a sheet of paper, plot the highs and lows of your life. Reflect on what God has been up to during your life. Go on to think about the future and make a note of your plans. Place them into God's hands; if possible (!) accepting that your plans for your life might not be God's plans.

Then Job replied to the LORD: 'I know that you can do all things; no plan of yours can be thwarted. You asked, "Who is this that obscures my plans without knowledge?" Surely I spoke of things I did not understand, things too wonderful for me to know.' Job 42:1–3

pray

Almighty God… thank you for revealing so many of your plans to us in the Bible – plans full of hope and promise. God, when the time is right, give me glimpses of the plans you have for me. But always remind me that you can do all things, and no plan of yours will be thwarted. Amen.

ponder
What dreams do you have for the future for yourself and your loved ones? Do you think that your dreams are the dreams that God would want you to have? If not, start dreaming about what you think God wants your future to look like.

TALK TOGETHER: DAYS 1–5

What do the people in our lives think about Jesus? How can we engage with these perceptions in order to lead them towards the authentic Jesus?

Day 1, John 1:1–5

In which areas of our lives do we sometimes feel inadequate? What could we do to help each other fight the disease of feelings of inadequacy?

Day 2, Genesis 1:26,27

Is it dangerous to differentiate between 'minor' and 'major' sins? Do we find ourselves doing this? Do we need to take all sin more seriously?

Day 3, Genesis 4:7

What are some of the benefits of sharing, rather than hoarding, our blessings? What examples could we share from our own experiences?

Day 4, Genesis 12:2,3

What bad situations has God used in our lives to get us to where he wants us? How can we help those who have lost sight of the 'light at the end of the tunnel'?

Day 5, Genesis 50:19–21

DAY 6: MORNING

beyond the wilderness

Be careful that you do not forget the LORD** your God ... who brought you out of Egypt, out of the land of slavery. He led you through the vast and dreadful wilderness ... He gave you manna to eat in the wilderness, something your ancestors had never known, to humble and test you so that in the end it might go well with you.** Deuteronomy 8:11a, 14b–16

Post-famine, Joseph's family settled in Egypt and after living there for 400 years they had multiplied – a lot! God's plan of making Abraham's descendants into a great nation was taking shape. As time went by the pharaohs forgot why the Israelites were there and became concerned that they were becoming too numerous and might take over. In order to control them, Pharaoh forced them into slavery.

God heard the cries of his people and sent Moses to lead them out of Egypt, shape them into a nation and take them to the Promised Land. It should have been a short journey, but because of their disobedience and lack of faith they were in the desert for 40 years before they finally, under the leadership of Joshua, entered the Promised Land.

During the Israelites' wilderness years they experienced many hardships, but they also experienced God's provision in awesome ways. Times of wilderness and transition can be fraught with challenges and difficulties. But they can also be a time of learning and an opportunity to experience God, and his provision, in new ways. When we find ourselves in a wilderness, perhaps what's most important is that we keep heading forwards.

pray

Faithful God… thank you for the journey you are taking me on. When I think that you've lost the map, remind me of the journey you took the Israelites on and how you shaped them and provided for them en route. Help me to keep walking forwards with you, and not turn back or sit down in a strop. Amen.

ponder

Do you find yourself in a wilderness or transition period at the moment? What do you think God might be doing in you, to you, and for you, because of it?

chat

If you're going through a transition period at the moment, speak to someone about it. Be honest about how you're feeling and invite them to give you advice. If you're not going through a transition period at the moment, but know someone who is, invite them to share their experience with you.

write

Find (or make) a luggage label and write a sentence from today's passage which seems most relevant to you right now. Then attach it to a bag you often carry about.

action

When you make a journey today, go a different way than you usually do; maybe even take a detour. For example, take the scenic route to the supermarket, walk through the park on the school-run, take a different mode of transport to work. Pay attention to your different surroundings, and be awakened by them.

DAY 6: EVENING

Give thanks to the LORD, for he is good.
His love endures for ever.
Give thanks to the God of gods.
His love endures for ever ...
to him who alone does great wonders,
His love endures for ever ...
who spread out the earth upon the waters,
His love endures for ever...
to him who led his people through the wilderness;
His love endures for ever ...
Give thanks to the God of heaven.
His love endures for ever.
Psalm 136:1,2,4,6,16,26

pray
Loving God… thank you for your goodness, your love and your provision. Sometimes I struggle to see these qualities in you and sometimes I feel alone and scared. But help me know in my heart, mind and soul that your love does endure for ever. Amen.

ponder
Instead of counting sheep, make a note of all the examples you know of God's enduring love – in the Bible, in your own life and in the lives of those you love.

DAY 7: MORNING

the laws of the land

These are the commands, decrees and laws the LORD** your God directed me to teach you to observe in the land that you are crossing the Jordan to possess, so that you, your children and their children after them may fear the L**ORD** your God as long you live by keeping all his decrees and commands that I give you, and so that you may enjoy long life.** Deuteronomy 6:1,2

As God took his people out of slavery in Egypt, through the wilderness and into the Promised Land, he shaped them into a nation. They had known only slavery, now they would be free. They could do whatever they liked. But think about it; is total freedom in this sense a good thing? I think not.

Is a game of football more enjoyable with rules and a referee or without rules and a referee? Is it best for a pet dog to be restricted to the house and garden or to be able to wander off, alone, onto the busy road?

Boundaries are good for us; society wouldn't work without them. God didn't give the Israelites lots of rules to spoil their enjoyment of life. In fact, the opposite is true, he gave them lots of rules so they could live a good life, in community with each other and God.

As Christians, our relationship to the Law is different from that of the Israelites entering the Promised Land. However, Jesus tells us we need to take the Law seriously (Matthew 5:17-20), and the Bible contains plenty of instructions that we should follow. Remember, they're there for our own good.

pray

Creator God… thank you for all the instructions you have provided us with – to enrich, not diminish my life. Make me eager to learn your ways. Help me humbly accept that I don't always know best and that you do. Thank you for having my best interests at heart. Amen.

ponder

How would your life be worse, if there were no rules or instructions? Think about that while you're driving, at the bank, cooking food or playing a game.

chat

Have a conversation with someone about the laws that exist in your country. Ask the person which one law they would remove from the law books and which one law they would add. If appropriate ask them what impression they have of the laws in the Bible.

write

If you press the F1 button on a computer, you can access the help menu – the gateway to your computer's instruction manual. Either write 'F1' on a label and stick it on the front cover of your Bible, or write 'When you need help with life, turn to the Bible' and stick it above the F1 button of your computer.

action

Identify one of the Ten Commandments (Exodus 20:1–17) that you most struggle to follow. Plan how you are going to consciously follow that commandment today. At the end of the day, reflect on how you did and how you could do even better tomorrow.

DAY 7: EVENING

'Teacher, which is the greatest commandment in the Law?'
Jesus replied: '"Love the Lord your God with all your heart
and with all your soul and with all your mind." This is the
first and greatest commandment. And the second is like
it: "Love your neighbour as yourself." All the Law and the
Prophets hang on these two commandments.'
Matthew 22:36–40

pray
*Loving God… thank you for providing such a succinct summary of
your Law. May the words 'Love God' and 'Love others' reverberate
around my mind, sink deep into my heart and saturate my soul,
then through my actions, let them spring forth from every fibre of
my being. Amen.*

ponder
What are you going to do tomorrow to demonstrate your
love for both God and others?

atonement

'He [Aaron] is to cast lots for the two goats – one lot for the Lord and the other for the scapegoat. Aaron shall bring the goat whose lot falls to the Lord and sacrifice it for a sin offering. But the goat chosen by lot as the scapegoat shall be presented alive before the Lord to be used for making atonement by sending it into the wilderness as a scapegoat.' Leviticus 16:8–10

If someone damages something that belongs to you it's going to cost somebody something! In order to fix the damage either the person who did the damage, a third party (ie an insurance company) or you have to pay.

While in the wilderness, God introduced a series of rituals the Israelites were to follow to recognise the seriousness of sin, the holiness of God and the need for reconciliation. At the heart of this system was the Day of Atonement, a day that was all about paying the price in order to fix the damage.

For the Israelites, a third party (two goats), paid the price. One goat was sacrificed and its blood was shed. As the animal's blood was shed, life left its body. That's the consequence of sin – it destroys life and carries a death sentence. The priest would then lay his hands on the other goat while the people confessed their sins. It would then be released into the wild. This is where we get the word 'scapegoat' from and it symbolises how God removes the life-destroying sin from his people and places it on another.

For us, it's not a third party that pays the price: it is God himself. The victim pays up. We cause the damage, but we don't pay the repair bill.

pray

Holy God… I recognise the seriousness of my life-destroying disobedience. Thank you that I do not have to pay the unaffordable price to repair this damage. As the Israelites placed their sin on a goat, as I confess my sin, I place it on your Son, thanking you for sending him to be my scapegoat. Amen.

ponder

What's more unfair: that God punishes sin or that he takes the punishment onto himself, so we don't have to pay the price for the damage we've caused?

chat

You might not realise it, but you probably frequently have conversations that involve the idea of 'atonement'! Watch, listen to or read the news and find a story that involves questions like, 'Who should pay to fix this problem?' Then, discuss the story with someone.

write

Confess your sins by writing them on something that you could use as a symbolic 'scapegoat'. For example, a sheet of toilet paper you could then flush down the toilet or, if you live by the sea, in the sand, to be washed clear by the incoming tide.

action

If someone has damaged something of yours lately, let them off! Or have you wronged somebody lately, either in word or deed? Make atonement for your wrong by putting things right with this person.

... for all have sinned and fall short of the glory of God, and all are justified freely by his grace through the redemption that came by Christ Jesus. God presented Christ as a sacrifice of atonement, through the shedding of his blood – to be received by faith. He did this to demonstrate his righteousness, because in his forbearance he had left the sins committed beforehand unpunished ... Romans 3:23–25

pray

Jesus my Saviour… I thank you for the grace you have shown me. May you help me comprehend more fully what it means to be forgiven and reconciled to God, not by my own attempts at fixing the damage, but because of what you achieved for me when you shed your blood on the cross. Amen.

ponder

Is there someone who has wronged you? How can you take the initiative to demonstrate grace and start the process of forgiveness and reconciliation?

DAY 9: MORNING

forwards and backwards

No sooner had Gideon died than the Israelites again prostituted themselves to the Baals. They set up Baal-Berith as their god and did not remember the LORD their God, who had rescued them from the hands of all their enemies on every side. They also failed to show any loyalty to the family of Jerub-Baal (that is, Gideon) in spite of all the good things he had done for them. Judges 8:33–35

There's a pattern in the Old Testament. God does something amazing so his people worship and obey him and things go well – they move forwards. But, as time goes on they forget about God, become disobedient and things don't go so well – they move backwards. When things have become really bad, they cry out to God begging him to help them.

God hears their desperate cries and does something amazing. So his people worship and obey him and things go well – they move forwards. But, as time goes on they forget about God, become disobedient and things don't go so well – they move backwards. When things have become really bad, they cry out to God begging him to help them.

Nowhere is this pattern more evident than in the book of Judges, which covers the period after the Israelites had entered the Promised Land, but before they had a king.

Before we criticise the Israelites, we must take a look at ourselves. We can be the same. We go to a Christian festival, read a good book, experience a miracle and we move forwards with God. But as time goes by we drift away and begin to move backwards, until we have another close encounter with God.

pray

Faithful God… I'm sorry for the times I forget about you and drift away. Thank you that you never forget about me. Help me become more aware of the amazing things you are doing all the time. Make me more alert to your Spirit as you seek to keep nudging me forwards. Amen.

---

ponder

What common threads exist between the times you've moved forwards with God? Then, ponder the common threads at times you've moved backwards.

---

chat

Arrange to meet a trusted friend and chat to them about what causes you to move forwards and what causes you to move backwards in your relationship with God. Ask them to suggest ways that will ensure you spend more time moving forwards rather than backwards. Invite them to pray for you.

write

In big letters, write the words 'Don't forget God.' Then display them somewhere prominent, for example, above your front door, beside your computer, or on the ceiling above your bed.

action

While listening to a song, press the 'rewind' button every 30 seconds or so. Alternatively, while watching a DVD, press the 'rewind' button every five minutes or so. It will be frustrating! In your frustration, relate this to the times you move backwards instead of forwards with God.

DAY 9: EVENING

Not that I have already obtained all this, or have already arrived at my goal, but I press on to take hold of that for which Christ Jesus took hold of me. Brothers and sisters, I do not consider myself yet to have taken hold of it. But one thing I do: forgetting what is behind and straining towards what is ahead, I press on towards the goal to win the prize for which God has called me heavenwards in Christ Jesus.
Philippians 3:12–14

pray
Heavenly Father… I not only want to keep looking forwards, I want to keep heading forwards. Please help me to do so. When I begin to slow, give me the energy to keep going. When I fall over, pick me up. And, when I start heading in the wrong direction, grab me and turn me around. Amen.

ponder
What has God got planned for you in the future? As you fall asleep, imagine what the future might hold for you if you keep moving forwards with God.

DAY 10: MORNING

a king like everyone else

But the people refused to listen to Samuel. 'No!' they said. 'We want a king over us. Then we shall be like all the other nations, with a king to lead us and to go out before us and fight our battles.' When Samuel heard all that the people said, he repeated it before the Lord. The Lord answered, 'Listen to them and give them a king.' 1 Samuel 8:19–22a

The Israelites were different from the other nations around them – they didn't have a king, because God was their king. However, they wanted a king like everyone else. Their first king was a man called Saul and things didn't go too well, because Saul disobeyed God.

A king is someone who leads and requires submission from his followers. You need to consider who or what is your king. Who or what sets the direction of your life? Who or what has the most influence over you? Who or what is in control?

Too often we sing 'Jesus is Lord' (another way of saying 'Jesus is King') on a Sunday, but for the rest of the week we sing a very different song. Some of us sing 'I am king', others sing 'My ambition is king' or 'My peers are king', while others sing 'Money is king' or 'My happiness is king'.

Like it or not we are all followers and none of us is immune to outside influences. Therefore, like the Israelites, we have to decide whether God will be our king, or whether we want a king like other people have.

pray

King Jesus… it's so easy to be like everyone else, but give me the strength to be different. It is my desire to submit to you, my king; it's just that I find it so hard to do! Reveal to me why you are the best king, the best direction-setter, the best influencer and the most qualified person to be in control of my life. Amen.

ponder

Who or what is in the driving seat of your life? How would your life be different if you submitted to Jesus as your king 24/7?

chat

Have a conversation today about who the key influencers and trendsetters are in society. In what way is their influence positive or negative? If possible, go on to discuss whether the church (or Jesus) is still influential in the world today.

write

If you drive a car, write the words 'Jesus is King' or 'Make sure Jesus is in the driving seat' (or something along those lines) on a sticky label and attach it to your steering wheel.

action

Make a list of the people and things that you think have too much (and/or a negative) influence over you. Then, throughout today, set aside a few minutes for each person and thing on your list. During those minutes, get yourself into a submissive position (eg kneeling), and reflect on how your life would be different if you placed Jesus above these other influencers.

DAY 10: EVENING

**'God opposes the proud but shows favour to the humble.'
Submit yourselves, then, to God. Resist the devil, and he
will flee from you. Come near to God and he will come near
to you.** James 4:6b–8a

pray
*Almighty God… when I think I know best, remind me that you know
better. Teach me, and guide me, in the ways of humility. Give me
both the humility and the courage to submit to you and your ways.
My desire is to live my life close to you; help my steps align with your
steps. Amen.*

ponder
Imagine time stood still and you could go for a walk around
your life with Jesus. (Like in a superhero movie when the
hero stops time, and can walk around altering things!) As
you walked around your place of work/study, your home,
your church, your social activities, what do you think Jesus
would have to say?

TALK TOGETHER: DAYS 6–10

What have been some of the most significant transition periods of our lives? Can we identify where God was and what he was up to during these times?

Day 6, Deuteronomy 8:11a,14b–16

What boundaries did our parents establish for us which at the time we disliked considerably, but in hindsight are extremely grateful for?

Day 7, Deuteronomy 6:1,2

How does it make us feel about God, ourselves, and everyone else around us, that Jesus paid the price and fixed the damage for us?

Day 8, Leviticus 16:8–10

What have been the causes of our major leaps forwards and drifts backwards? How can we help each other to keep moving forwards?

Day 9, Philippians 3:12–14

For each of us, what one thing would be different in our lives if we allowed Jesus to remain in the driving seat 24/7?

Day 10, James 4:6b–8a

DAY 11: MORNING

a man after God's own heart

But the LORD said to Samuel, 'Do not consider his appearance or his height, for I have rejected him. The LORD does not look at the things people look at. People look at the outward appearance, but the LORD looks at the heart.' ... So Samuel took the horn of oil and anointed him [David] in the presence of his brothers. 1 Samuel 16:7,13a

Saul's kingship was a bit of a debacle. Next came David, who is described as a man after God's own heart (1 Samuel 13:14). David's time as king was much more successful; however, it wasn't without its hiccups! King David walked close to God, and by and large obeyed his ways. But that wasn't always the case, and David's life featured some grave sins with heartbreaking consequences. Perhaps most importantly, David never forgot it was God who made him king; he relied on God rather than his own strength, and when he sinned he always turned back to God.

David was very different from Saul. For one, the Bible tells us that Saul was 'traditional' king material – he was 'as handsome a young man as could be found ... a head taller than anyone else.' (1 Samuel 9:2). David, on the other hand, was just a boy who looked after the animals. No one thought he looked special. But he was God's choice.

Chances are you're more like David than Saul – this might bother you, but don't let it. Remember God looks at the heart, not the outward appearance. Today, people spend a lot of time and effort making sure they keep up a good appearance. When you're tempted to keep up with the Joneses, remember what's really important.

pray

All-knowing God… help me focus my attention on developing a heart that pleases you rather than an image that impresses other people. Make me stand out not because of my image but because of my Christ-like character. Amen.

ponder

Have you got a heart and character that pleases God, or do you need to do some work on the inside? If so, what needs to be done?

chat

Talk to some people about what they value in a work colleague, friend or partner. The likelihood is that certain character traits will be high on the list, while things to do with the outward appearance will be lower down. Pose the question: why do we worry so much about our outward appearance?

write

On a sticky note or small sheet of paper write the words, 'The Lord does not look at the things people look at. People look at the outward appearance, but the Lord looks at the heart.' Then, attach it to a mirror, next to, or to replace, the passage from day 2.

action

At some point today, go out of the house deliberately not worrying about your outward appearance! For example, go to work without make-up, or go to the shops in your slippers. (If you've got an important meeting at work, perhaps you should postpone this idea for a day or two – don't turn up in ripped jeans!)

DAY 11: EVENING

He [David] said: 'The LORD is my rock, my fortress and my deliverer; my God is my rock, in whom I take refuge, my shield and the horn of my salvation. He is my stronghold, my refuge and my saviour – from violent people you save me.' 2 Samuel 22:2,3

pray

God my rock… in times of trouble encourage me to follow the example of King David. Prompt me to come to you, so you can protect me. When the storms of life are raging all around me, remind me not to face them alone, but to take refuge in you, and then for us to tackle them together. Amen.

ponder

Remember a time when you found refuge in God during difficult circumstances. What did it feel like? Turn your thoughts into a prayer of gratitude.

the wisdom of Solomon

The proverbs of Solomon son of David, king of Israel: for gaining wisdom and instruction; for understanding words of insight; for receiving instruction in prudent behaviour, doing what is right and just and fair; for giving prudence to those who are simple, knowledge and discretion to the young – let the wise listen and add to their learning, and let the discerning get guidance ... The fear of the LORD is the beginning of knowledge, but fools despise wisdom and instruction. Proverbs 1:1–5,7

After David came Solomon. Things began well for Solomon, but he was easily influenced, and as a result he drifted away from God and turned to other gods.

King Solomon is most well known for his wisdom. Towards the beginning of his time as king, he had a dream in which he asked God to give him wisdom so he could govern his people well (1 Kings 3:9–15). It impressed God that he asked for wisdom instead of wealth or a long life, so God granted him his desire – along with wealth and long life.

Do you desire wisdom? Are you a wise person? It's important to realise that being wise is not the same as being intelligent or knowledgeable. You can be a rocket scientist or a pub quiz champion and still be a fool!

The internet provides us with an overwhelming amount of information. If we sift through that information we'll find knowledge. However, knowledge should not be the end. We shouldn't learn just to gain knowledge. The crucial step is the next one. We need to put knowledge into practice – that's what it means to be wise.

pray

Father God… increase my desire for wisdom. Give me the humility I need to ask for help and to accept the guidance of others. Make me eager to learn from every person I encounter and every experience I have. May my search for wisdom begin and end with you. Amen.

ponder

What areas of your life could do with an injection of wisdom? Where could you go to gain the wisdom you require?

chat

Arrange to have a coffee with someone you consider to be wise. If you are in need of guidance or advice, take the opportunity to talk to them about this. If not, just chat to them about whatever comes up, but as they talk, be actively learning from them.

write

Place a stack of books somewhere prominent. Then, write the words, 'Let the wise listen and add to their learning, and let the discerning get guidance' on a sheet of paper and attach it to the stack of books.

action

Start today by purchasing a small notepad. During the day (and for the rest of the week), try to learn something from every situation you experience and everyone you meet. At regular intervals, record in your notepad what you're learning. (Instead of buying a notepad you could just use the back of your diary or do it electronically.)

DAY 12: EVENING

Whoever derides their neighbour has no sense, but the one who has understanding holds their tongue. A gossip betrays a confidence, but a trustworthy person keeps a secret. For lack of guidance a nation falls, but victory is won through many advisors. Proverbs 11:12–14

pray

Loving God… increase my eagerness to learn from your Word and may your Holy Spirit guide me in the ways of wisdom. Shape me into a person of integrity and help me approach every conversation and situation in a wise and godly manner. Amen.

ponder

Think about the people you will encounter and the situations you'll face tomorrow and consider how you will be able to display wisdom. Then, pray.

DAY 13: MORNING

remembered as a faithful follower

Hezekiah trusted in the Lord, the God of Israel. There was no one like him among all the kings of Judah, either before him or after him. He held fast to the Lord and did not stop following him … he was successful in whatever he undertook. He rebelled against the king of Assyria and did not serve him. 2 Kings 18:5–7

Not long after Solomon died civil war broke out and Israel was divided into two – a northern kingdom (Israel) and a southern kingdom (Judah). In the period that followed the forwards and backwards pattern continued. Occasionally there would be a good, God-fearing king who would take the people forwards. Far more often there were bad kings who would take the people backwards.

Hezekiah was one of the few good kings, and this obituary-like passage gives him a glowing report. Perhaps a slightly sombre thought, but what do you want your obituary to say? What do you want to be remembered for?

Not many people get to read their own obituary, but Alfred Nobel did! When his brother died, the newspaper printed the wrong obituary. It focused on how he had created dynamite and as a result was responsible for more death and destruction than anyone who had ever lived. Alfred Nobel was horrified and decided to do something to change how he would be remembered. He used his wealth to establish an award to recognise people who work for peace – the 'Nobel Peace Prize'. His plan to rewrite his obituary worked: today, most people associate his name with peace, not destruction.

Do you need to rewrite your obituary?

pray

Eternal God… my years on earth are few; help me to use them wisely. I desire to be a positive influence on every person, and in every situation, that makes up my life. Above all else, I want to be remembered as someone who faithfully followed you. Amen.

ponder

If you died sometime soon, what would your obituary say? Are you happy with this? If not, what changes do you need to make?

chat

Have a conversation with someone about how they would like to be remembered after they've died. What do they want their obituary to say?

write

Cut a sheet of paper into the shape of a grave stone. Then write the following words from Hezekiah's 'obituary' on it, 'He held fast to the Lord and did not stop following him.' There might be specific things that you want to be remembered for, but in general terms that's a pretty good obituary line to be aiming for!

action

Alfred Nobel made a change: with the wealth he made from war, he invested in peace. Do one thing today that changes a negative into a positive, a weakness into a strength. For example, if you usually say something unkind to a colleague, say something kind to them instead. If you usually frown, smile. If you usually ignore someone, go out of your way to talk to them.

So then, brothers and sisters, stand firm and hold fast to the teachings we passed on to you, whether by word of mouth or by letter. May our Lord Jesus Christ himself and God our Father, who loved us and by his grace gave us eternal encouragement and good hope, encourage your hearts and strengthen you in every good deed and word.

2 Thessalonians 2:15–17

pray

Faithful God… in all the activities, joys, challenges and busyness of everyday life, help me to remember your teachings. Help me to stand firm, give me the courage I need to follow you, and never let me forget the hope you give. Amen.

ponder
In what area of your life do you need to receive strength, encouragement and hope at the moment? Ask God to provide you with all three.

the whispers of God

The Lord said, 'Go out and stand on the mountain in the presence of the Lord, for the Lord is about to pass by.'

Then a great and powerful wind tore the mountains apart and shattered the rocks before the Lord, but the Lord was not in the wind. After the wind there was an earthquake, but the Lord was not in the earthquake. After the earthquake came a fire, but the Lord was not in the fire. And after the fire came a gentle whisper. When Elijah heard it, he pulled his cloak over his face and went out and stood at the mouth of the cave.

Then a voice said to him, 'What are you doing here, Elijah?'
1 Kings 19:11–13

God's people were disobedient. However, God didn't give up on them – instead he sent prophets, his spokespersons, to warn the people that if they didn't change their ways and turn back to God they would get themselves into all sorts of trouble. Elijah was one of these prophets.

As we read the Old Testament it can be hard to accept that the God of the Israelites is the same God we seek to worship and serve today. God in the Old Testament is so obvious: his actions are so visible (eg Moses and the burning bush; the parting of the Red Sea). Yet, this passage is encouraging – God doesn't just speak and reveal himself through mighty acts; he whispers. Does God speak and intervene in the affairs of the world less today than in biblical times? No. It's not God who has changed; it's us. Perhaps we're just less tuned in to what God is doing. We need to listen to the whispers of God.

pray

Almighty God… help me to recognise what you are doing in the world and in my life. Enliven my senses to your presence and enable me to glimpse your work, and hear your whispers. Amen.

ponder

Is God trying to get your attention at the moment? Watch and listen. What is God trying to show and say to you?

chat

Have a conversation with someone you know who believes that God exists in some form or another. Find out what they think God is up to in the world at the moment and whether they think God speaks to people. Chat to them about what you think God might currently be doing and saying.

write

Make a sign which says, 'Quiet please: God is whispering to me.'

action

At some point today it's likely that you'll be surrounded by frantic activity and noise. For example, in a city centre, a school playground, a queue, or even in your own house. Take a step back, and as the noise carries on around you listen out for the whispers of God. What is he up to?

DAY 14: EVENING

The LORD is my shepherd, I lack nothing. He makes me lie down in green pastures, he leads me beside quiet waters, he refreshes my soul. Psalm 23:1–3a

pray

God my shepherd… I often seem to wander off by myself; please help me stay close to you. I want you to care for me, to guide me and protect me. Prompt me to make sure I spend plenty of time in 'green pastures' and beside 'quiet waters' so you can restore my soul. Amen.

ponder
Imagine yourself lying somewhere quiet – on a beach, in a field or by a river. Ask God to comfort your heart, still your mind and restore your soul.

DAY 15: MORNING

(un)faithfulness

When the Lᴏʀᴅ began to speak through Hosea, the Lᴏʀᴅ said to him, 'Go, marry a promiscuous woman and have children with her, for like an adulterous wife this land is guilty of unfaithfulness to the Lᴏʀᴅ' ... The Lᴏʀᴅ said to me, 'Go, show your love to your wife again, though she is loved by another man and is an adulteress. Love her as the Lᴏʀᴅ loves the Israelites, though they turn to other gods and love the sacred raisin cakes.' Hosea 1:2; 3:1

Prophets didn't just include illustrations in their sermons to communicate their message; they turned their lives into a living illustration.

The message God wanted Hosea to communicate was that his people were like an unfaithful woman, who went from one man to another. To illustrate this, God actually asked Hosea to marry an adulterer. And, when she was unfaithful, he didn't abandon her; he didn't even just forgive her and welcome her back – he actually went to her and invited her to return to him! In doing so, Hosea was communicating to God's people that while they were unfaithful to him, he was faithful to them. Despite the fact that they had 'got into bed' with other gods, he still loved them and wanted them back.

Thinking of ourselves as adulterers is uncomfortable, but it's an accurate description. God loves us faithfully, but how often are we unfaithful to him? How often do we make something or someone else the focus of our worship? Imagine what the consequences would be if we treated our partner like we treat God?

Despite our unfaithfulness, God is always ready to welcome us back.

pray

Faithful God… I am sorry for the times I commit adultery against you. My actions are inexcusable, but I thank you that you are always ready and willing to forgive me. Help me be faithful and work at our relationship. Amen.

ponder

In what ways have you been unfaithful to God lately? What do you need to do to put more effort into yours and God's 'marriage'?

chat

When a marriage runs into difficulties its wise to get 'couples' counselling'. If you know your relationship with God requires some attention, arrange to meet with someone you trust. Ask them to provide you with some 'couples' counselling'.

write

As a circle is endless, so a wedding ring represents that love and faithfulness within marriage should endure for ever. Tie a piece of string around your finger to remind you of your relationship with God. You could write a set of marriage vows. They might contain some of the promises that God makes to you in the Bible, and the promises you'd like to make to God.

action

If you have a wife, husband, girlfriend or boyfriend, do something 'above and beyond' to show them how much you love them. Have a romantic meal together, buy them a gift, go for a walk or write a love letter. As you make this effort in this relationship, remind yourself to make an effort also in your relationship with God.

Because of the Lord**'s great love we are not consumed, for his compassions never fail. They are new every morning; great is your faithfulness.** Lamentations 3:22,23

pray
Loving God… thank you for your love and faithfulness. Thank you for not giving up on me even when I give up on you. I'm sorry for the times I've let you down today, but thank you for being merciful. As I wake tomorrow remind me of your compassion for me and help me walk in the way of faithfulness. Amen.

ponder
Think of times during your life that God's compassion and faithfulness towards you have been obvious. Turn these memories into prayers of gratitude.

TALK TOGETHER: DAYS 11–15

When it comes to the idea of 'keeping up with the Joneses', where are we weak? How can we help each other focus on what's really important?

Day 11, 1 Samuel 16:7,13a

Are there any situations that we are facing at the moment that could do with an injection of wisdom? Perhaps we could advise one another.

Day 12, Proverbs 1:1–5, 7

When you die, what would you like the first line of your obituary to say?

Day 13, 2 Kings 18:5–7

How did you find listening out for the whispers of God? Was it easy to find the necessary stillness and/or silence? What did God say to you?

Day 14, 1 Kings 19:11–13

What one thing do we each need to do to put more effort into our relationship with God?

Day 15, Hosea 1:2; 3:1

DAY 16: MORNING

faith in action

'I hate, I despise your religious festivals; your assemblies are a stench to me. Even though you bring me burnt offerings and grain offerings, I will not accept them. Though you bring choice fellowship offerings, I will have no regard for them. Away with the noise of your songs! I will not listen to the music of your harps. But let justice roll on like a river, righteousness like a never-failing stream!' Amos 5:21–24

Amos was another prophet, with another challenging message. His prophecy begins with God's judgement on Israel's neighbours. The Israelites would have loved this: criticising their neighbours was one of their most favourite pastimes and not much made them happier than seeing God punish them.

However, their enjoyment didn't last for long. God then went on to point out their own faults, and the list is quite long. God's people should be setting an example to the nations around them, but they're as bad, if not worse, than their neighbours.

It appears that the Israelites were going through the motions of worship, but they were not really worshiping God. They said they were following him, but they weren't. God wanted them to put their words into action.

We need to take note of these stern words. Firstly, we shouldn't be critical of others until we've first examined ourselves. Secondly, does our faith result in action? The Bible makes it quite clear that God is a fan of justice, and helping the poor and marginalised was a top priority for Jesus. Is your heart beating in time with God's? Are your priorities the same as Jesus'?

pray

God in heaven… may my worship be acceptable to you. Help me to worship you not just with words, but with actions. Increase my desire for justice and align my priorities with yours.

> **ponder**
> What are some of the common things you criticise other people for? How many of these criticisms should first be directed at yourself?

chat

A common complaint against Christians is that we're hypocrites. Chat to a few colleagues or friends about this. Do they agree? If any of the people you speak to have been on the receiving end of Christian hypocrisy, apologise on behalf of Christians.

write

On a slip of paper write the words, 'Away with the noise of your songs! I will not listen to the music of your harps. But let justice roll on like a river, righteousness like a never-failing stream!' and attach it to your radio, iPod or other music-playing device. Then, go one day without listening to music. Instead, when you would usually listen to music, think about how you can bring a little more justice and righteousness into the world.

action

Make a list of five things you could do today to put your faith into action. As the day progresses, tick them off as you successfully complete each action.

What good is it, my brothers and sisters, if someone claims to have faith but has no deeds? Can such faith save them? Suppose a brother or a sister is without clothes and daily food. If one of you says to them, 'Go in peace; keep warm and well fed,' but does nothing about their physical needs, what good is it? In the same way, faith by itself, if it is not accompanied by action, is dead. James 2:14–17

pray

Lord Jesus… increase my compassion and desire to help those in need. Increase my wisdom to know how I can best help. Increase the amount of connection between my intentions, words and actions. Amen.

ponder

Who do you know who could do with your help at the moment? Instead of just wishing them well, how could you actually help them?

discipline not destruction

'For many years you were patient with them. By your Spirit you warned them through your prophets. Yet they paid no attention, so you gave them into the hands of the neighbouring peoples. But in your great mercy you did not put an end to them or abandon them, for you are a gracious and merciful God.' Nehemiah 9:30,31

God kept sending prophets to urge his people to repent of their disobedience and turn back to him. He warned his people that if they didn't turn back to him they would be defeated and captured by their enemies. They didn't repent, so God, as ever, kept his word. In 722 BC the nation of Israel was invaded by the Assyrians, the cities were destroyed and the people were taken captive. The southern nation of Judah was captured by the Babylonians in 586 BC. Jerusalem was destroyed and all the young people were taken to Babylon as prisoners.

It's important to realise that God's purpose in exiling his people was not destruction but discipline. He didn't completely wipe out the Israelites; instead he taught them valuable lessons. It can be hard for us to get our heads around discipline at a national level like this; however, we can learn important lessons from the experience of the Israelites.

When we face difficulties and challenges it may or may not be God disciplining us. Either way, God can always use the tough times to shape us into the people he wants us to be. When we do experience God's discipline we must remember that he does it because he loves us and wants the best for us.

pray

Father God… help me realise that my actions have consequences.
I pray that I will pay attention to the warnings you send my way.
But, when I do get it wrong, I thank you that you love me enough to
discipline me. Amen.

---

ponder

Have you ever felt like you've been in exile? Have you ever experienced God's loving discipline? How did experiences such as these help you in the long run?

---

chat

As a child, what parental discipline did you most dread or prefer? Can you remember a specific time you were disciplined that has really benefited you? (Be aware that this might be a painful issue for some.)

write

Create a few small red triangular warning signs and put them in places where a warning is required. For example, if you think your television watching habits have the potential to pull you away from God, place a warning triangle by your television.

action

If you're a parent, and have a place where you usually send your child when they've done something wrong (eg a 'naughty step'), go and spend some time there yourself! Use the time to say sorry to God and think about how he wants you to act differently in the future. If you're not a parent, go to a place which you associate with discipline from your own childhood.

'My son, do not make light of the Lord's discipline, and do not lose heart when he rebukes you, because the Lord disciplines the one he loves, and he chastens everyone he accepts as his son.' Endure hardship as discipline; God is treating you as his children ... No discipline seems pleasant at the time, but painful. Later on, however, it produces a harvest of righteousness and peace for those who have been trained by it.' Hebrews 12:5b–7a, 11

pray

Loving God… thank you that I mean so much to you that you are prepared to take the time and make the effort to discipline me and point me in the direction I should go. I pray that I will be a quick learner! Amen.

ponder

If you were to discipline yourself right now, what faults would you point out and how would you go about addressing them?

DAY 18: MORNING

living as a foreigner

By the rivers of Babylon we sat and wept when we remembered Zion. There on the poplars we hung our harps, for there our captors asked us for songs, our tormentors demanded songs of joy; they said, 'Sing us one of the songs of Zion!' How can we sing the songs of the Lord while in a foreign land?" Psalm 137:1–4

God didn't completely destroy the Israelites; a remnant remained and they found themselves living in a foreign land, as exiles. They no longer lived surrounded by people who were like them. The people they now lived amongst had very different values, beliefs and practices. Ring any bells?

The United Kingdom used to be described as a 'Christian country'. However, today, it's more likely to be described as a 'secular-with-a-mix-of-faiths country'. Our experience is more similar to the Jewish remnant living in Babylon, than to the Jewish people living in Jerusalem.

This affects a lot of things! It makes following God harder as we often find ourselves swimming against the tide. It affects how we engage with politics, the government and society at large. We are foreigners in our own country! As a result, we need to decide (as Daniel had to) which customs and practices we can embrace, and which ones we need to avoid.

We should not accept everything, but neither should we just complain or criticise; we should be offering an alternative. We are called to 'sing the songs of the Lord while in a foreign land.' We should be singing a different song.

pray

King Jesus… continually remind me that first and foremost I am a citizen of heaven. When I feel like a misfit, remind me that I am! Teach me to sing a different song from the people around me, and I pray that my song is catchy and that others will want to learn the song I'm singing. Amen.

ponder

What would happen if you started singing a different song from those around you? What do the 'songs of the Lord' sound like?

chat

Discuss the following question with a few people: if your life were to be made into a movie, what are some of the songs you'd like to be part of the soundtrack?

write

If it's possible to set a 'welcome message' on your music-playing device, set it to say, 'How can we sing the songs of the Lord while in a foreign land?' Alternatively, write this verse on a sheet of paper and place it next to your music collection.

action

Listen to a piece of music that you think will help you 'sing the songs of the Lord while in a foreign land'. It doesn't have to be a 'Christian song'. Listen to it a few times, perhaps humming it, or singing it to yourself. Whatever you do, just make sure that song will be playing in your head for the rest of the day. Then, throughout the day, make sure the lyrics influence your actions.

Dear friends, I urge you, as foreigners and exiles, to abstain from sinful desires, which war against your soul. Live such good lives among the pagans that, though they accuse you of doing wrong, they may see your good deeds and glorify God on the day he visits us. 1 Peter 2:11,12

pray

Heavenly Father… give me the courage to be different. Give me the strength to swim against the tide when that is what is necessary. Help me sing a song that will fill people with hope. Help me live a life that will give people a glimpse of you. Amen.

ponder
When was the last time someone noticed and commented that you were 'different'? What opportunities might you have tomorrow to be noticed? Pray that this will give you an opportunity to point people to God.

return and restoration

'**Remember the instruction you gave your servant Moses, saying, "If you are unfaithful, I will scatter you among the nations, but if you return to me and obey my commands, then even if your exiled people are at the farthest horizon, I will gather them from there and bring them to the place I have chosen as a dwelling for my Name.'** Nehemiah 1:8,9

God had a plan for his people; he didn't destroy them when they were disobedient, and he didn't forget about them while they were in exile. Within a few generations the exiles were able to return home to rebuild their capital city, Jerusalem. Ezra and Nehemiah led the return, and urged the people to learn from their past mistakes and submit themselves to God and his Law.

If you've ever been sick for an extended period of time, you've probably experienced the feelings associated with return and restoration. The joy of subsiding pain and returning strength, that mix of fear and excitement as you prepare to return to work. It's like the 'first-day-of-work-after-a-holiday feeling' except you're leaving something bad rather than good behind!

If you have drifted away from God, or if the circumstances of life have taken you away from him, know that his desire is for you to return and begin the, not always easy, process of restoration. The first step is to return to him, to confess and start following him once more. As you think about the challenges and opportunities that lie ahead, fear and excitement are inevitable emotions. But remember, God doesn't want you to return to your past, he wants you to return to him, so he can restore you, so that together you can move into the future.

pray

Gracious God… I'm sorry for the times I drift away from you, whether because of my disobedience or because of the circumstances of life. Thank you that returning is always an option. Restore me, and lead me into the future. Amen.

ponder

Think about a time you had those 'returning to reality' feelings (eg after a holiday, sickness or even the weekend). What did you feel and why were you feeling those things? Relate these feelings to returning to God.

chat

Discuss with someone whether they've ever been to a school reunion. What was it like? How did they feel before they went? Are they pleased they went? If the person you're talking to hasn't been to a school reunion, ask them whether they would like to!

write

Imagine a reunion. For example, a couple reuniting after a business trip, best friends reuniting after 30 years, or a parent and child reuniting after an argument. You may even like to sketch the scene. Then, write down the words you associate with the reunion you are imagining.

action

Is there something in your life that needs restoring, for example, an object, your garden, or a relationship? If so, begin the process of restoration today. Alternatively, have you got something that belongs to someone else, for example, a book, DVD or item of clothing? If so, return it.

DAY 19: EVENING

'But while he was still a long way off, his father saw him and was filled with compassion for him; he ran to his son, threw his arms round him and kissed him. The son said to him, "Father, I have sinned against heaven and against you. I am no longer worthy to be called your son." But the father said to his servants, "Quick! Bring the best robe and put it on him. Put a ring on his finger and sandals on his feet. Bring the fattened calf and kill it. Let's have a feast and celebrate. For this son of mine was dead and is alive again; he was lost and is found."' Luke 15:20b–24a

pray
Father God… thank you for your compassion and forgiveness. Thank you that despite all the times I walk away from you – in little ways each day, and sometimes in big ways – you are always waiting to welcome me home. Amen.

ponder
Do you know anyone who has walked away from God? Pray for them and think about how you could help them make the journey home.

DAY 20: MORNING

waiting

We also have the prophetic message as something completely reliable, and you will do well to pay attention to it, as to a light shining in a dark place, until the day dawns and the morning star rises in your hearts. 2 Peter 1:19

Waiting. Whether waiting in a queue at the Post Office or waiting to hear the results of a medical test, waiting is rarely a pleasant experience!

The Israelites had some pretty dark days; however, they also had a glimmer of hope. The prophets had spoken about a Messiah, someone who would come and make everything OK. They waited in the dark, for the light.

Waiting is a common theme in the Bible: Abraham had to wait for a son; Joseph had to wait for his dream to come true; the Israelites had to wait to enter the Promised Land, and then they had to wait for the Messiah to come. However, just think what God taught them, and how he shaped them, through the process of waiting.

Today we are not waiting for the Messiah in the same way the Israelites were. However, we still experience waiting. We wait for God to fulfil his promises for the future that we read in the Bible. We wait to experience what we believe God has planned for our lives. We wait for God to work in the lives of those we love. We wait for the light to begin shining in dark places.

We spend so much time waiting you would have thought we'd be good at it! However, most of us are not. We need to learn to wait well.

pray

Faithful God… give me the patience I require to wait for your plans to come to pass. Give me the wisdom I require to learn the lessons you are trying to teach me as I wait. And give me the faith I require to know that your plans always prevail. Help me to not only accept, but embrace, the value of waiting. Amen.

ponder

What are you waiting for at the moment? What might God be trying to teach you through this waiting period?

chat

Take time today to speak to someone who is experiencing a difficult wait at the moment. Perhaps they are waiting for test results, waiting for a child to come home from serving in a war zone or waiting to complete a house sale. Encourage them and offer to pray for them.

write

We have come to expect things instantly. When we shop on the internet, we want the goods to arrive the next day. The internet is getting faster and faster, but we'd still like it to go even faster. Write the words 'God's promises are not like fast food' and attach them to your microwave.

action

Whenever you find yourself waiting today, spend the time thinking about God's faithfulness, and praying. In fact, if you have the chance, increase your waiting time! Join the longest queue in the supermarket, arrive at the doctor's ten minutes early or don't select next day delivery when you shop online.

DAY 20: EVENING

I waited patiently for the LORD; he turned to me and heard my cry. He lifted me out of the slimy pit, out of the mud and mire; he set my feet on a rock and gave me a firm place to stand. He put a new song in my mouth, a hymn of praise to our God. Many will see and fear the LORD and put their trust in him. Psalm 40:1–3

pray

Lord God… when I'm waiting, help me not to become restless, but instead find rest in you. Remind me that my future, and the future of those I love, is in your hands. Help my faith to be strengthened in times of waiting, not weakened. Give me the courage to trust you. Amen.

ponder

If you're waiting for something at the moment, replace your anxious thoughts with confident ones that stem from the knowledge that whatever happens God is with you and that you can trust in him.

TALK TOGETHER: DAYS 16–20

As a group, what could we do to ensure that we put our faith into action – particularly when it comes to issues of justice?

Day 16, Amos 5:21–24

What have been some of our positive experiences of discipline, from parents, teachers, sport coaches, employers, God, or even the police?!

Day 17, Hebrews 12:5b–7a,11

As Christ-followers, in what ways should we blend in and cooperate with society around us, and in what ways should we stand out and make a noise?

Day 18, Psalm 137:1–4

Have any of us got stories we are willing to share of how we've experienced God's restoration work in our lives?

Day 19, Nehemiah 1:8,9

Are any of us waiting for anything at the moment? How are we finding the experience of waiting? How can we support one another in our waiting?

Day 20, Psalm 40:1–3

DAY 21: MORNING

God is with us

'She will give birth to a son, and you are to give him the name Jesus, because he will save his people from their sins.' All this took place to fulfil what the Lord had said through the prophet: 'The virgin will conceive and give birth to a son, and they will call him Immanuel' (which means 'God with us'). Matthew 1:21–23

In the Bible we discover that God makes a lot of promises, but do you know what the promise that God makes most frequently is? It's the promise, 'I will be with you.' We do not worship and serve a distant God, but one that is close, one that is involved, one that is with the people that he created.

Nowhere is this more clearly evidenced than in the person of Jesus. God came and lived amongst us. He couldn't become any bigger or more powerful to impress us, so he became smaller and weaker to attract us.

What makes this more incredible is that God wants to be with us even though we so often abandon him. God wants to be with us even though we have messed up everything he so lovingly gave us. Sin has ruined everything and has caused God so much pain. Yet God didn't remain in heaven yelling at us to sort things out. No. He came down to earth and he lived amongst all our mess.

He didn't say, 'I'll come and be with you once you've sorted out your mess.' Instead he said, 'I'll come and be with you and help you sort out your mess.'

pray

Ever-present God… thank you. Thank you. Thank you. Thank you that you are always with me. Thank you that you don't abandon me even when I abandon you. Thank you that you are willing to help me sort out the mess I so often make of my life. Thank you that you came to earth to save me. Amen.

ponder
Does the thought that God is always with you scare you or encourage you? Pay attention to the presence of God in the world today.

chat
Many people, perhaps even most, believe in some notion of 'God'. Chat with a work colleague, friend, or family member today about what sort of 'God' they believe in. Take the opportunity to introduce them to the God that you believe in.

write
Buy and eat a packet of ready-salted crisps. As you eat them, remember the promise God has made to be always with us. Then pin the empty packet to a pin board. Why? In the Old Testament, salt was used as a symbol of the promises made by God to his people.

action
The question, 'Where is God when it hurts?' is a common one. However, God has asked us to be his representatives on earth, so part of the answer to that question depends on where we are when people are suffering. Today, display the love of God in a practical and tangible way to someone who is suffering.

DAY 21: EVENING

In your relationships with one another, have the same
mindset as Christ Jesus: who, being in very nature God, did
not consider equality with God something to be used to his
own advantage; rather, he made himself nothing by taking
the very nature of a servant, being made in human likeness.
And being found in appearance as a man, he humbled
himself by becoming obedient to death – even death on a
cross! Philippians 2:5–8

pray

*Jesus… your humility is astounding. The reason why you did what
you did is equally astounding. I thank you for what you did and
for the example you have given us. In the light of my faults, my
weaknesses and my mistakes, who am I not to be humble? Please
nurture a Christ-like attitude within me. Amen.*

ponder

Think about Jesus and what he was like. Think about how
you can become more like Jesus. How would that affect
your relationships with other people?

DAY 22: MORNING

identity

At that time Jesus came from Nazareth in Galilee and was baptised by John in the Jordan. Just as Jesus was coming up out of the water, he saw heaven being torn open and the Spirit descendingon him like a dove. And a voice came from heaven: 'You are my Son whom I love; with you I am well pleased.' At once the Spirit sent him out into the wilderness, and he was in the wilderness for forty days, being tempted by Satan. Mark 1:9–13a.

The Bible doesn't tell us that much about Jesus' childhood or his years as a young adult – only a few incidents are recorded. It's not until he is nearly 30 that he makes his dramatic entrance on to the public stage.

Given the lack of details regarding Jesus' formative years, there's plenty of speculation as to how he coped with finding out that he was the Son of God. Did he always know? Was it something that he discovered slowly? Did he struggle to come to terms with his identity? We'll never know. However, what we do know is that at his baptism his identity is clearly revealed, 'You are my Son whom I love; with you I am well pleased.'

After his baptism Jesus went into the wilderness and was tempted. Knowing his identity undoubtedly helped him resist the temptation he faced. The same is true for us. Knowing our identity will help us resist temptation. Because of what Jesus achieved for us through his life, death, resurrection and ascension, if we choose to associate ourselves with him, we become children of God. We can own God's words, 'You are my child whom I love; with you I am well pleased,' for ourselves.

pray

Father God… I wear many different labels and there are many aspects of my identity. Continually remind me that above all I am your child and this should affect every other aspect of my identity. Help me be secure in my identity as one of your children. Amen.

ponder

What temptations are you facing at the moment? How should knowing that you are a child of God help you resist these temptations?

chat

As well as being tempted to do things, we can also be tempted to think things. And sometimes it's what we think about ourselves that is the problem. We can be tempted to think we are insignificant, worthless or a failure. This can lead to our feeling insecure, and consequently make us even more vulnerable to temptation. Speak to a trusted friend about your insecurities and/or temptations. Invite them to counsel you and pray for you.

write

Find a photograph of you when you were a child. Display it somewhere prominent, and write the words 'I am a child of God' on it, or next to it.

action

Read Psalm 51:1–12 and then take an extra long bath, shower, or if you're at work or out and about, go into a washroom and wash your hands and face. As you do so ask God to wash your sins away, to make you secure in your identity as one of his children and help you resist temptation.

DAY 22: EVENING

No temptation has overtaken you except what is common to mankind. And God is faithful; he will not let you be tempted beyond what you can bear. But when you are tempted, he will also provide a way out so that you can endure it. 1 Corinthians 10:13

pray

Jesus my Saviour… you know what it feels like to be tempted. You are a friend, a brother even, with experience, so let me learn from you. Give me the strength I need to stand up in the face of temptation. And when I'm tempted give me the common sense to walk away. Amen

ponder

Briefly think about the temptations you face, but don't dwell on them. Instead, dwell on how your life would be better if you walked away from them.

DAY 23: MORNING

commander's intent

'The Spirit of the Lord is on me, because he has anointed me to proclaim good news to the poor. He has sent me to proclaim freedom for the prisoners and recovery of sight for the blind, to set the oppressed free, to proclaim the year of the Lord's favour.' Luke 4:18,19

Early on in his public ministry, Jesus read this passage from Isaiah. He went on to say that he was the fulfilment of this prophecy. That certainly caused a stir!

This was Jesus' mission statement – it succinctly reveals to us what his mission to earth is all about. Or put another way, it was his 'Commander's Intent' (CI).

For the military, planning missions is a very important task, yet it is highly problematic! They know exactly what they need to achieve, but planning is difficult because there are so many variables.

Therefore, the military developed the CI approach. At the top of every mission plan, the Commander's Intent is stated in the clearest terms possible. For example, 'Secure the western quarter of the city'. Underneath there is a detailed plan; however, if the plan falls apart, everyone remains clear on what needs to be done.

Jesus had a clear CI. Perhaps we should as well. We never know what life will throw at us; many days don't go according to plan. Maybe a CI would help us ensure that, whatever happens to us, we don't lose sight of what we're meant to be doing. And, if we're following Jesus, surely our CI should be similar to his.

pray

Creator God… you have lovingly given me the gift of life, you have mercifully given me the gift of salvation, and you have gracefully given me skills, resources and opportunities. Help me to use everything you have given me as you would want me to. Amen.

ponder

What does God want you to do and how does he want you to do it? Don't think specifically, think generally. In all situations, what does God want us to do?

chat

Introduce the idea of CI to someone, and discuss what you would each include in a CI for your lives. (If you prefer, you could use the idea of a 'mission statement' instead.)

write

Take some time out today to write a CI for your life. As well as looking at Luke 4:18,19, you may also like to look at some other passages. For example, Matthew 6:33, 22:36–40 and 28:18–20.

action

In Jesus' Commander's Intent there is a clear emphasis towards the poor and needy, although spiritually speaking we are all poor, imprisoned, blind and oppressed without Jesus. Therefore, make sure you do at least one thing today that puts your CI into action in a way that benefits someone who is in need.

DAY 23: EVENING

Let the message of Christ dwell among you richly as you teach and admonish one another with all wisdom through psalms, hymns and songs from the Spirit, singing to God with gratitude in your hearts. And whatever you do, whether in word or deed, do it all in the name of the Lord Jesus, giving thanks to God the Father through him.
Colossians 3:16,17

pray

Almighty God… may my life be saturated with the words of Christ. May my heart always be full of gratitude. May my mind be occupied with godly thoughts. And in everything I do – the seemingly mundane things and the seemingly significant things – may I do everything in a way that gives you glory. Amen.

ponder

What will you be doing tomorrow? How can you do all these things, and the things that take you by surprise, in a manner that gives God glory?

bringing people to Jesus

Some men brought to him a paralysed man, lying on a mat. When Jesus saw their faith, he said to the man, 'Take heart, son; your sins are forgiven.' At this, some of the teachers of the law said to themselves, 'This fellow is blaspheming!' Knowing their thoughts, Jesus said, '... Which is easier: to say, "Your sins are forgiven," or to say, "Get up and walk"? But I want you to know that the Son of Man has authority on earth to forgive sins.' So he said to the paralysed man, 'Get up, take your mat and go home.' Then the man got up and went home. Matthew 9:2–7

These men were desperate to get this paralysed man to Jesus. In the Gospels of Mark and Luke we learn that they couldn't get him to Jesus in the conventional way, because of the crowds. So they went up on to the roof, removed a section of it, and lowered him down in front of Jesus. It's not surprising that Jesus was impressed with their faith!

How eager are you to bring your friends to Jesus? The first step is intercession: we should pray on behalf of our friends. If someone you know is having a tough time, pray for them. The next steps might include telling them that you're praying for them, talking to them about Jesus and inviting them to church.

Jesus didn't just heal the paralysed man physically, he also healed him spiritually. Just as Jesus was concerned with the whole person, so should we be.

Those there, including the paralysed man and his companions, probably came to see Jesus the healer and wise teacher in action. However, when Jesus revealed himself as God, they got a whole lot more than they bargained for!

pray

Jesus the healer… give me the courage I need to offer to pray for people. Give me the boldness to tell people about what you've done in my life and what you could do in theirs. Give me the confidence to bring people to you. Amen.

ponder
Think of a few people you could bring to Jesus. How could Jesus help them?

chat

If during a conversation with someone today you find out that they are struggling with something at the moment, offer to pray for them. You could, if you're feeling really bold, do it with them there and then! Otherwise, tell them you'll pray for them during your own prayer time or ask if it's OK for you to pray about their situation with your small group.

write

A group of men lowering a paralysed man through a roof is a pretty strong image! Draw a quick sketch of this (stick men will be fine), then around the sketch write the names of people you need to bring to Jesus. Alternatively, you could draw pictures of what bringing them to Jesus might look like.

action

Scroll through all your contacts on your mobile phone and every time you get to someone you think you should pray for, stop and pray for them. Then, send them a text to let them know they're in your thoughts and prayers. Also say that if they would like you to do something for them, they should just ask.

DAY 24: EVENING

Now to him who is able to do immeasurably more than all we ask or imagine, according to his power that is at work within us, to him be the glory in the church and in Christ Jesus throughout all generations, for ever and ever! Amen.
Ephesians 3:20,21

pray

God Almighty… remind me that when I pray I'm praying to the Creator of the universe! Remind me that you can do so much more than I could possibly dream of. Please open my eyes and ears so that I don't miss out on witnessing and experiencing your power that is at work all around me. Amen.

ponder

Think of someone you know who is very resistant to the things of God. Ask God to do something amazing in their life. Then, pay attention to what he's doing!

DAY 25: MORNING

friend of sinners

'Why do you eat and drink with tax collectors and sinners?' Jesus answered them, 'It is not the healthy who need a doctor, but those who are ill. I have not come to call the righteous, but sinners to repentance.' Luke 5:30b–32

Jesus spent a lot of time with people that no self-respecting religious person would associate with; he was often accused of being a friend of sinners. When was the last time that accusation was made against you? Because, if you're seeking to be Christ-like, it should be something people are accusing you of!

Jesus wants to save sinners. He wants to save sinners from themselves. He wants to save sinners from life-destroying sin. He wants to save sinners from a hopeless eternity.

You might be uncomfortable with labelling people 'sinners' and it's probably unwise to go around addressing people as 'Sinner Bob' or 'Sinner Jane'! However, we need to acknowledge the seriousness of sin: otherwise the good news of Jesus doesn't make much sense! If people don't realise there's a problem, they're not going to be interested in the solution.

We need to spend time with 'sinners'. We need to love them like Jesus loved them and we need to help them encounter Jesus for themselves. That doesn't mean we have to approve of their sin. Doctors spend a lot of time with sick people, but that doesn't mean they approve of sickness!

pray

Friend of sinners… I thank you that you love sinners and came to save people who were lost. When I'm feeling superior and holier-than-thou, remind me that I too am a sinner – saved only by your grace. Please put a lot of sinful people in my life; help me love them and direct them to you. Amen.

ponder

What is your attitude towards people who don't yet know Christ? Is it a Christ-like attitude? If not, how do you need to see people differently?

chat

Chatting is an essential part of friendship. Today, chat to as many people as possible – colleagues, friends, family members, even strangers. Don't do so with an agenda (there's no 'discussion question' today!), just chat. The only pointer is to make sure the focus of the conversation is on them – their interests, their news and their needs.

write

Find a plaster, and on it write the words, 'It is not the healthy who need a doctor, but the sick.' Stick the plaster somewhere appropriate – maybe even on your body!

action

Is there someone in your life who you are always clashing with? Perhaps it's someone that has a very different lifestyle from yours – maybe it's a lifestyle that you consider to be sinful. Do something nice for that person today – buy them a cup of coffee, make them cake or compliment them on what they are wearing.

DAY 25: EVENING

'Suppose one of you has a hundred sheep and loses one of them. Doesn't he leave the ninety-nine in the open country and go after the lost sheep until he finds it? And when he finds it, he joyfully puts it on his shoulders and goes home. Then he calls his friends and neighbours together and says, "Rejoice with me; I have found my lost sheep." I tell you that in the same way there will be more rejoicing in heaven over one sinner who repents than over ninety-nine righteous persons who do not need to repent." ' Luke 15:4–7

pray

Seeking God… when people lose their way and wander far from you, your response is not to forget about them, it's to go looking for them. Thank you for finding me when I get lost. I ask that you will help me see people through your eyes and empower me to join you in your search. Amen.

ponder

Think of a few people you know who God is looking for at the moment. Pray that these people will realise they are lost and want to be found.

TALK TOGETHER: DAYS 21–25

'At what times in our lives have we felt the presence of God particularly strongly? How can these times help us when God doesn't feel so close?

Day 21, Matthew 1:21–23

Do we consider ourselves to be children of God? How do you think we would see ourselves, and each other, differently if we truly grasped this?

Day 22, Mark 1:9–13a

What were the key components of the 'Commander Intent statments' we wrote this week? What are the common themes that exist between them?

Day 23, Colossians 3:16,17

Who are some of the people in our lives that we need to bring to Jesus? How can we make sure we remember to pray for one another as we seek to do this?

Day 24, Matthew 9:2–7

Do we spend enough time (or perhaps too much) with 'sinners'? How can we ensure that we remain faithful to Christ and don't get ensnared by sin?

Day 25, Luke 5:30b–32

the kingdom of God

Then Jesus asked, 'What is the kingdom of God like? What shall I compare it to? It is like a mustard seed, which a man took and planted in his garden. It grew and became a tree, and the birds perched in its branches ... It is like yeast that a woman took and mixed into about thirty kilograms of flour until it worked all through the dough.' Luke 13:18,19,21

The kingdom of God was at the heart of Jesus' teaching. However, it's an idea that is often misunderstood. When Jesus started talking about the kingdom of God, many people were excited. The Jews had been waiting a long time for the Messiah – someone they believed would usher in God's kingdom by freeing them from the Romans and establishing his eternal rule from a throne in Jerusalem.

Jesus disappointed many people. He didn't overthrow the Romans and instead of sitting on a throne wearing a golden crown he was nailed to a cross wearing a thorny crown. But Jesus' mission wasn't a failure. It's just that God's kingdom was very different from what the Jews expected. He hadn't come to free the Jews from the Romans; he had come to free everyone from sin. He didn't come just to rule the Jews, but to teach everyone how to live in God's kingdom.

Today, many Christians also misunderstand the kingdom of God; they think it's primarily about the future – the place they will go when they die. However, the kingdom of God is a present reality as well as a future hope. God's kingdom is under construction; we can experience it in part now, and in full later. Whenever we submit to the rule and reign of God, his kingdom breaks through.

pray

King Jesus… I submit to your rule and reign and I want to play my part in extending your kingdom here on earth. My desire is for my life to be like yeast – for it to have a kingdom impact on everyone I encounter. Amen

---

ponder

Think about the values of the kingdom of God; what's important, what's not? What impact would you have on those around you if you lived these values?

---

chat

Discuss with people whether they think Christians (or people of any faith for that matter) should keep their faith private, or whether faith should be public. If the people you talk to think that faith should be kept private, challenge them to think about all the public good churches and individual Christians do – actions which are motivated by faith.

write

Plant a seed, and on the pot write, 'The kingdom of God is like a mustard seed.' As you watch it grow, reflect on whether the kingdom of God is becoming increasingly visible in your life, and what impact this is having on the lives of those around you.

action

Buy a newspaper. Firstly, mark all the stories that contain glimpses of the kingdom of God. Secondly, pick a few stories and consider how things would be different if God's kingdom was more visible here on earth.

'... your kingdom come, your will be done, on earth as it is in heaven.' (Matthew 6:10)

pray

God in heaven… I'm looking forward to spending eternity with you in heaven. But remind me that eternity starts now. Please help me do what I can to bring heaven to earth. I begin submitting every area of my life to your rule and reign, so that I may be a good ambassador of your kingdom. Amen.

ponder

Think of three things you can do tomorrow that will bring a little bit of heaven to earth. That is, God's will being done in a particular situation.

DAY 27: MORNING

forgiveness

Then Peter came to Jesus and asked, 'Lord, how many times shall I forgive my brother or sister who sins against me? Up to seven times?' Jesus answered, 'I tell you, not seven times, but seventy-seven times.' Matthew 18:21,22

When Jesus said we should forgive someone 77 times he wasn't placing a limit on forgiveness; he was implying the opposite – there is no limit, we should keep on forgiving. He went on to tell a story.

A servant owed his master a lot of money. He couldn't pay, so he begged for mercy, and the master cancelled the debt. The servant went out, and found someone who owed him a little money. He also couldn't pay, so he also begged for mercy, but he was shown no mercy from the man who had just received mercy. The message is clear – God has forgiven us much and at a great cost; therefore we should forgive others.

If we don't forgive, ill-feeling not only lingers, it can take hold and spread like cancer. We must recognise that not forgiving someone usually does more damage to us than to the person we refuse to forgive. If we don't forgive, it's us who are burdened with a weight and it's us who becomes a breeding ground for bitterness. It's us who run the risk of this bitterness damaging our other relationships as well. By not forgiving someone, the person you're punishing the most is yourself.

pray

Forgiving God… thank you for forgiving me. I thank you that every time I come to you needing forgiveness for yet another thing I have done wrong you are willing to forgive me. Nurture within me the forgiving attitude you have towards me, so I can have that attitude towards those who wrong me. Amen.

ponder

Who do you need to forgive? As you think about them, think about how God has forgiven you, and how much that forgiveness cost him.

chat

Discuss with a few people what things they would find very difficult, to forgive. If possible find out about people's experiences of forgiveness and chat about why it's important to forgive.

write

At school, were you ever made to write 'lines' as a punishment? To illustrate the repetitive nature of forgiveness, and to drill the idea deep into your mind, grab a sheet of paper and write, 'I must always forgive' at least 20 times.

action

Is there someone you need to forgive? Today, take the first steps to begin the process of forgiveness. A few comments before you take action. Firstly, you might be thinking, 'But they haven't asked for forgiveness'. Remember, it was God who made the first move; we should be proactive. Secondly, forgiveness does not always lead to reconciliation; however, it's an essential step in the process of reconciliation. Thirdly, it's going to take time.

Therefore, as God's chosen people, holy and dearly loved, clothe yourselves with compassion, kindness, humility, gentleness and patience. Bear with each other and forgive one another if any of you has a grievance against someone. Forgive as the Lord forgave you. And over all these virtues put on love, which binds them all together in perfect unity.
Colossians 3:12–14

pray

God of compassion… please help me deal with the bitterness, anger and resentment I hold towards other people. Help me let go. As I get dressed tomorrow morning, may I also clothe myself with compassion, kindness, humility, gentleness and patience. Amen.

ponder
Think of a person you struggle with, perhaps someone who's hurt you. Think about how you can show them compassion, kindness, humility, gentleness and patience.

the Last Supper

… the Lord Jesus, on the night he was betrayed, took bread, and when he had given thanks, he broke it and said, 'This is my body, which is for you; do this in remembrance of me.' In the same way, after supper he took the cup, saying, 'This cup is the new covenant in my blood; do this, whenever you drink it, in remembrance of me.' For whenever you eat this bread and drink this cup, you proclaim the Lord's death until he comes. 1 Corinthians 11:23b–26

The meaning of the cross is so complex that we will never fully fathom it. Yet at the same time, there's a simplicity about it that children seem to be able to grasp more easily than adults.

There's a story about how NASA invested years, and millions of dollars, inventing a pen that would allow them to write in space – difficult given that it's gravity that causes ink to flow. When they succeeded they proudly announced their achievement to the world. The Canadians sent NASA a note, 'Congratulations, but why don't you just use a pencil like we do?'

There's certainly nothing wrong with wanting to explore our questions, study theology and increase our understanding of God. But, in our desire to delve deeper into the complexities of the Christian faith, we must never lose sight of the simplicity at the heart of its message. Jesus' body was broken and his blood shed so our sins could be forgiven and we might be reconciled to God.

Jesus gave his followers an extremely simple and tangible way to remember the significance of his death on the cross – sharing bread and wine together – two basic, everyday commodities.

pray

Crucified Saviour… as I wrestle with my theological questions and in my desire to increase my understanding, help me not to lose sight of the central message of the cross – a message of love, forgiveness and reconciliation. Amen.

ponder

How should Jesus' broken body and shed blood affect how you live your life? Every time you eat and drink today, remember Jesus' death on the cross.

chat

The symbol of the cross is undoubtedly the most well known Christian symbol. Ask a few people what words they associate with the cross. Go on to find out whether they think the cross is the most appropriate symbol for Christianity. If they were given the task of designing Christianity's new 'logo' what symbol would they choose and why?

write

Place some bread and a bottle of wine (or a carton of grape juice or glass of blackcurrant squash) in the centre of your table. In addition, you could write out today's passage and place it next to the bread and wine.

action

If possible, share the Lord's Supper with someone today. Now, churches approach the Lord's Supper in different ways; therefore, do this in a way that is respectful to the beliefs of your church and in a manner that you are comfortable with.

DAY 28: EVENING

'Whoever wants to be my disciple must deny themselves
and take up their cross daily and follow me. For whoever
wants to save their life will lose it, but whoever loses their
life for me will save it. What good is it for someone to gain
the whole world, and yet lose or forfeit their very self?'
Luke 9:23b–25

pray
*Lord Jesus… forgive me for my self-centredness. Give me the
courage to take up the cross each day. Help me surrender my
dreams and ambitions to your will. Make my life less about me and
more about you and other people. Amen.*

ponder
Are you in danger of trying to 'gain the whole world yet
forfeit your soul'? How would remembering to pick up the
cross of Christ each day help you?

unanswered prayer

'Father, if you are willing, take this cup from me; yet not my will, but yours be done.' An angel from heaven appeared to him and strengthened him. And being in anguish, he prayed more earnestly, and his sweat was like drops of blood falling to the ground. Luke 22:42–44

Do you ever feel that your prayers are falling on deaf ears? You pour out your heart to God and are greeted with the sound of silence. Unanswered prayer is the cause of much anxiety and pain. It can be heart-breaking.

Jesus knows how you feel. In the Garden of Gethsemane Jesus knew what was about to happen and he pleaded with God to stop it. This prayer was not answered in the way Jesus wanted it to be. He was still crucified. However, this was not Jesus' only prayer. He also prayed, 'Yet not my will, but yours be done.' Jesus trusted his Father and was willing to submit himself to his will. Do you trust God enough to pray this prayer for yourself?

God may not have answered Jesus' first prayer in the manner in which Jesus was hoping for, but that's not the same as saying that God didn't listen or respond. When Jesus asked for 'this cup to be taken away', God's answer was no, but he responded by sending an angel to strengthen him. For reasons we may never know, God doesn't always take away our problems; however, he will always strengthen us and be there to help us.

pray

Father God… thank you that nothing we say to you is ever ignored. Increase my level of trust so that I am able to pray, 'Yet not my will, but yours be done.' When you do not answer my prayers in the way I desire, give me the humility to accept it and the strength to keep going. Amen.

ponder

Think back to times when God hasn't answered your prayers in the way you wanted. With the benefit of hindsight, are you pleased that God doesn't always give you what you ask for?

chat

Ask a few people today, who as far as you know don't go to church or follow Jesus, whether they pray. Find out what sort of things they pray for, why they pray, and whether they have experienced any answers.

write

Get a cup and write the words of verses 42 and 43 on a label or slip of paper. Then, attach the words to the cup. Over the coming days, hold this cup when you pray.

action

Do you know someone who is currently experiencing the pain of unanswered prayer? Do something that will strengthen and encourage them. For example, spend time listening to them, send them some flowers, write them a letter, or take them out for lunch.

DAY 29: EVENING

Do not be anxious about anything, but in every situation, by prayer and petition, with thanksgiving, present your requests to God. And the peace of God, which transcends all understanding, will guard your hearts and your minds in Christ Jesus. Philippians 4:6,7

pray
Compassionate God... when everything seems to be going wrong, help me remember the things I do have that I can be grateful for. Help me give my anxious thoughts to you, and in return receive your peace. Please direct the feelings of my heart and the thoughts of my mind. Amen.

ponder
You probably don't need to be told to think about the things you're anxious about! As you think about them, place them one by one into God's hands.

DAY 30: MORNING

ashamed or shy?

About an hour later another asserted, 'Certainly this fellow was with him, for he is a Galilean.' Peter replied, 'Man, I don't know what you're talking about!' Just as he was speaking, the cock crowed. The Lord turned and looked straight at Peter. Then Peter remembered the word the Lord had spoken to him: 'Before the cock crows today, you will disown me three times.' And he went outside and wept bitterly. Luke 22:59–62

This incident is both shocking, and, if you're anything like me, all too familiar. Perhaps you've never lied outright about your church-going habits, your faith in Christ or your beliefs in general, but have you ever found yourself redirecting the conversation, avoiding the subject or telling only half the story?

You've started a new job and on Monday morning your colleagues are chatting about what they've been up to over the weekend. You tell them about the gardening and the barbecue with friends but you fail to mention that you went to church Sunday morning.

Your friends are chatting about the antics of an over-zealous Christian character from a popular TV soap. You know where the conversation is heading, so you decide this is a good opportunity to head to the bathroom.

Why do we do this? Is it because we're ashamed of Jesus? More likely it's because we're ashamed of the Christian religion. Is it because we're shy? Perhaps we're scared of what people will think of us or scared that we'll say something stupid and put them off Christianity even more! Whatever the reason, we need to sort it. If we don't, we're missing out on life-changing, Jesus-encountering conversations!

pray

Jesus… please help me to stop being such a wuss! Give me confidence to not only live my faith in public, but to talk about it. Help me walk towards conversations that could introduce people to you, not away from them. Amen.

ponder

Do you dodge opportunities that God gives you to talk about your beliefs? If so, why do you think this is? And, what can you do to stop doing it?

chat

Today, if your conversations head in a God-ward direction, don't change the subject. Seize the opportunity! Mention that you go to church, or talk about how your values stem from your faith. It's natural to talk about things that are important to you (for example, football, food, your children, music); therefore, it should be natural to include your faith in your conversations.

write

If you need to 'come out of the closet' as a Christ-follower, write out today's passage and attach it to the inside of your wardrobe door. Alternatively, you could write something like, 'Don't change the subject', or 'Make the most of every opportunity'

action

Do something today that might cause people to comment on your faith, ask questions about God, or at least begin to notice that you might be a Christian. For example, wear a cross lapel pin, read your Bible on the train, leave a copy of your church notice sheet on your desk, or put a fish sticker on your car.

DAY 30: EVENING

'You are the light of the world. A town built on a hill cannot be hidden. Neither do people light a lamp and put it under a bowl. Instead they put it on its stand, and it gives light to everyone in the house. In the same way, let your light shine before others, that they may see your good deeds and glorify your Father in heaven.' Matthew 5:14–16

pray

Light of the world… help me to shine more brightly. When people look at me may they notice that I'm a little bit different. I want my life to be a signpost that points people in your direction. Give me the courage I need to do this. Amen.

ponder
When might you be tempted to hide your light under a bowl tomorrow? What can you do to place it on a stand instead and point people to God?

TALK TOGETHER: DAYS 26–30

What glimpses have we had this week of God's kingdom? In what situations have we longed for God's will to be done on earth as it is in heaven?

Day 26, Matthew 6:10

What stories of forgiveness have made an impact on us? Are there stories from our own lives (of either received or given forgiveness) that we are able to share?

Day 27, Colossians 3:12–14

How would each of us present the gospel message in just one sentence?

Day 28, 1 Corinthians 11:23b–26

Can we think of times when we were pleased that God didn't answer our prayers in the way we asked him to? How have you come to terms with unanswered prayers?

Day 29, Luke 22:42–44

Do we sometimes hide our faith? Why do we do this? How can we support each other to become more obvious Christ-followers?

Day 30, Matthew 5:14–16

DAY 31: MORNING

in the shadow of the cross

'He committed no sin, and no deceit was found in his mouth.' When they hurled their insults at him, he did not retaliate; when he suffered, he made no threats. Instead, he entrusted himself to him who judges justly. 'He himself bore our sins' in his body on the cross, so that we might die to sins and live for righteousness; 'by his wounds you have been healed.' 1 Peter 2:22–24

At the heart of Christianity is Jesus Christ. The pinnacle of his life was his death and resurrection. It was a death like no other. His death changed everything: it was world-changing, heaven-and-hell-changing, and for those who choose to believe the message of the cross it is life-changing.

As we approach the cross, we catch a glimpse of God's mind-blowing love for us; Jesus suffered greatly and he did it for us. As we stand in its shadow, we can receive forgiveness of sin; we just need to come, believe and ask.

At the cross a great exchange takes place. Before we come to the cross we are guilty, yet because Jesus received our sentence, we go away acquitted. Before we come to the cross we are due to be punished, yet because Jesus took the punishment for us we go away having received the reward of righteousness and eternal life. Before we come to the cross we are slaves to sin, yet because Jesus paid the price for our release we go away free from sin. Before we come to the cross we are separated from God, yet because Jesus removes the barrier we go away reconciled to God.

pray

My Saviour… thank you for enduring the cross for me so that I might be forgiven. Thank you that there is a reward waiting for me, not punishment and for reconciling me to your Father. Help me live as a free person, and to avoid the trap of sin. Amen.

ponder

Throughout today think about the great exchange that took place at the cross. How is your life different because of the cross? What have you exchanged?

chat

Have a conversation with someone about the best exchanges they have ever made. For example, as a child swapping stickers or some other collectable item, part-exchanging a car, or selling junk from the loft so they could buy something they really wanted.

write

Draw (or make) a simple cross. Then, on the cross, write the words, 'He himself bore our sins in his body on the cross, so that we might die to sins and live for righteousness; by his wounds you have been healed.'

action

Exchange something in order to act out today's central idea. Sell something you don't use any more, and with the money buy something you really want. If you have some left over foreign currency, get it exchanged today. Swap an item of clothing with a friend. Alternatively, just take some time today to throw away some junk!

DAY 31: EVENING

For as high as the heavens are above the earth, so great is his love for those who fear him; as far as the east is from the west, so far has he removed our transgressions from us. As a father has compassion on his children, so the Lord has compassion on those who fear him. Psalm 103:11–13

pray

Compassionate God… thank you for your willingness to forgive sin. When I begin to dwell on my past transgressions, please remind me that you have removed them completely and taken them a long way away. Amen.

ponder

Is there some past (or present) transgression that you're struggling to put behind you? As you're thinking about it, ask God to forgive you and thank him that he takes it away. Now imagine handing this transgression to God and picture him taking it on foot or by bicycle/car/ferry/aeroplane a long way from you!

in the light of the empty tomb

We were therefore buried with him through baptism into death in order that, just as Christ was raised from the dead through the glory of the Father, we too may live a new life. For if we have been united with him in a death like his, we will certainly also be united with him in a resurrection like his. For we know that our old self was crucified with him so that the body ruled by sin might be done away with, that we should no longer be slaves to sin ... count yourselves dead to sin but alive to God in Christ Jesus. Romans 6:4–6,11

Too many Christians live in the shadow of the cross rather than in the light of the empty tomb. Yes, we're meant to come to the cross, stand in its shadow and confess our sins. However, we're not meant to stay there! We're meant then to go and live our lives in the light of the empty tomb. We come to the cross in order to put our sins to death, so that we can then live new lives. We share in Christ's death, so that we can share in his resurrection. We leave the old life behind, so that we can live a new life.

Imagine a couple are celebrating their 40th wedding anniversary and the husband gets a card for his wife and in it writes, 'Today we celebrate 40 years since we left our parents'. That card probably wouldn't receive a warm reception! Leaving your parents behind is an essential part of the marriage ceremony, but it's not the reason you get married; you leave your parents so that you can begin a new life as a couple.

Being a Christian is not just about leaving sin behind – it's about living a new life. We come to the cross so that we can move forward.

pray

Risen Saviour… thank you that I not only get to associate with your death, but also with your resurrection. Help me leave my old life behind so that I can move forward and live a new life. May I focus on following you, and living the life you want me to live. Amen.

ponder

Do you live in the shadow of the cross or in the light of the empty tomb? What should be the key features of life lived in the light of the empty tomb?

chat

Ask God to give you the courage to chat to someone about how Jesus has changed your life. Tell them about what your life was like before you knew Christ and what it is like now you're 'living in the light of the empty tomb'. Focus on why your life is better with Christ in it.

write

On a sheet of A4 paper write the word 'SIN' in pencil, so it fills the whole page. But don't press too hard! Then, get an eraser and rub out the word and place the sheet of paper somewhere obvious. Every time you look at it, remember that your 'new life' is like a blank sheet of paper; how are you going to fill it?

Action

Reflect on your life; is there something you need to stop doing? Decide to stop. However, if you just decide to stop, you probably won't succeed. You need to replace the old with something new. So as well as *stopping* something, *start* doing something. For example, stop eating chocolate, start eating fruit!

DAY 32: EVENING

Therefore, if anyone is in Christ, the new creation has come: the old has gone, the new is here! All this is from God, who reconciled us to himself through Christ and gave us the ministry of reconciliation ... We are therefore Christ's ambassadors, as though God were making his appeal through us. We implore you on Christ's behalf: be reconciled to God. 2 Corinthians 5:17,18,20

pray
Christ Jesus… I thank you that because of you I am a new creation. Each day reduce the old-without-Christ-me, and increase the new-with-Christ-me. Now I am reconciled to you, help me play my part in reconciling others to you. Amen.

ponder
Think about the newness of life in spring. Don't just think about what it looks like: think about the smells, the sounds and how it feels. Now imagine the changes that would take place in your life if it were springtime.

good news to tell

'Do not leave Jerusalem, but wait for the gift my Father promised, which you have heard me speak about. For John baptised with water, but in a few days you will be baptised with the Holy Spirit ... you will receive power ... and you will be my witnesses in Jerusalem, and in all Judea and Samaria, and to the ends of the earth.' Acts 1:4b,5,8

After Jesus' death and resurrection he appeared to lots of people, then within a few weeks returned to heaven, entrusting his followers to tell other people the good news. It was a big responsibility to give us humans – surely it was a risky strategy?!

Jesus had prepared the way. He had promised that after he returned to heaven he would send the Holy Spirit who would counsel, guide and empower Christ-followers with the task they had been given. When God's Spirit turned up (at Pentecost), it transformed and empowered a bunch of men, who had run away scared when Jesus was arrested, into seemingly fearless and definitely world-changing evangelists!

We have good news to be telling people! We like talking about good news. If we discovered a great restaurant, had a great holiday or if our child graduated, we'd be eager to tell everyone. But, are we that eager to tell people about the good news of Jesus? Jesus has entrusted you with a very important mission.

pray
Lord Jesus… thank you for giving me such good news to share. Give me opportunities to tell people about you, and give me courage to seize them. May your Holy Spirit empower me to get involved with the mission you have entrusted to your followers. Amen.

chat

There's too much bad news in the world! Therefore, inject some good news into the conversations you have today. Find out what good news there is in the life of the person you're conversing with and share good news from your life.

write

For Jesus' listeners Jerusalem was familiar territory, as, to a lesser extent, was Judea. Samaria was a hostile environment and 'the ends of the earth' were unknown! On a sheet of paper draw four concentric circles and label them (from the inside outwards), Jerusalem, Judea, Samaria, the world. Write the names of groups (or individuals) that each of these places represents for your own witnessing. For example, Jerusalem = family, Judea = close friends, Samaria = work. For 'the world' you may like to write down the names of missionaries you support (or know) who are living overseas.

action

God has provided us with his Holy Spirit to empower us to tell people the good news. As you're thinking about the Holy Spirit's power, use the opportunity to replace any batteries that need replacing, charge devices that need charging and change any light bulbs that need changing.

DAY 33: EVENING

Then Jesus came to them and said, 'All authority in heaven and on earth has been given to me. Therefore go and make disciples of all nations, baptising them in the name of the Father and of the Son and of the Holy Spirit, and teaching them to obey everything I have commanded you. And surely I am with you always, to the very end of the age.'
Matthew 28:18–20

pray
Father, Son and Holy Spirit… it's amazing that you invite me to have a relationship with you and entrust me to be involved in your work. When I am daunted by the task, remind me that you are always with me. Amen.

ponder
Who do you need to be talking to about the good news of Jesus? How could you go about discipling them in the ways of Jesus?

DAY 34: MORNING

a community of Christ-followers

They devoted themselves to the apostles' teaching and to fellowship, to the breaking of bread and to prayer. Everyone was filled with awe at the many wonders and signs performed by the apostles. All the believers were together and had everything in common. They sold property and possessions to give to anyone who had need. Every day they continued to meet together in the temple courts. They broke bread in their homes and ate together with glad and sincere hearts, praising God and enjoying the favour of all the people. And the Lord added to their number daily those who were being saved. Acts 2:42–47

While Jesus was on earth he planted the seed of an idea, an idea that would be a central component to this rapidly growing movement of Christ-followers. That idea was the church. These few verses provide us with an exciting and dynamic picture of what the early church was like.

There is much we can learn from the early church; however, we can't just attempt to replicate the early church, because the society we find ourselves in is very different from theirs. We need to learn from them, and then paint our own picture. We need to create a community of Christ-followers that can bring hope to today's world.

It seems that for many Christians church is like Marmite – they either love it or hate it! How you reflect on this passage will largely depend on your experience of church. However, whatever you do, try to be positive! Think of how a community of Christ-followers can nurture and encourage each other. Think of the opportunities that exist for churches to transform communities.

pray

Loving God… the church was your idea, and therefore it's a good idea! It is my desire to be part of a church that is transforming lives. Inspire me to play my part in making my church a healthy one. Amen.

ponder

If your church ceased to exist, would anyone in the community notice?

chat

In verse 47 it says that the early church, 'enjoy[ed] the favour of all the people'. Is that true of churches today? Find out! Speak to a few people about their perceptions of church and what the church is up to in the world. Think about what your church could learn from their comments (and maybe even chat to a leader).

write

Find a copy of your church notice sheet and write a verse or two from Acts 2:42–47 on it. For example, 'They devoted themselves to the apostles' teaching and to fellowship, to the breaking of bread and to prayer,' or 'All the believers were together and had everything in common,' or 'And the Lord added to their number daily those who were being saved'.

action

Arrange to meet up with someone from your church for coffee, lunch or a walk. There doesn't need to be an agenda for your time together. However, if you're normally negative about your church, focus on the positive. If you're normally pessimistic about your church's future, be optimistic!

DAY 34: EVENING

Let us hold unswervingly to the hope we profess, for he who promised is faithful. And let us consider how we may spur one another on towards love and good deeds, not giving up meeting together, as some are in the habit of doing, but encouraging one another – and all the more as you see the Day approaching. Hebrews 10:23–25

pray

Father God… when I doubt, give me the faith I need. When I feel like giving up, bring others to me to keep me going. Motivate and equip me to be an active member of my church. Ensure that I am someone who builds up the body of Christ, not tears it down. Help me encourage others. Amen.

ponder

Is there someone you haven't seen at church lately? Pray for them and make a mental note to contact that person tomorrow.

DAY 35: MORNING

gifted to play

For just as each of us has one body with many members, and these members do not all have the same function, so in Christ we, though many, form one body, and each member belongs to all the others. We have different gifts, according to the grace given to each of us. If your gift is prophesying, then prophesy in accordance with your faith; if it is serving, then serve; if it is teaching, then teach; if it is to encourage, then give encouragement; if it is giving, then give generously; if it is to lead, do it diligently; if it is to show mercy, do it cheerfully. Romans 12:4–8

Imagine what would happen if three players in a football team decided to sit down and watch the rest of the team play the game (perhaps even moaning about the rest of the team's performance). The team wouldn't be able to play to its full strength and it would be annoying for the other players. If you're part of a church, you're part of a team. You should be playing, not watching. If you're not playing your part, your church isn't going to reach its full potential.

Now imagine what would happen if the midfielder decided to play in goal, and the goalkeeper decided to play up front and the striker decided to play in defence. That wouldn't go so well either! We're all good at different things; that's how God designed us – so we need to play to our strengths.

The Bible reveals that as well as our natural talents, the Holy Spirit gives us gifts. The purpose of these gifts is to build up the church – to help it be all it can be. If you're not using your gifts, you won't be fulfilled, the church won't be doing all it could be doing, and as a result other people will lose out.

pray

Almighty God… I want to be a participant in what you're doing through the church, not a spectator. Help me to embrace the things I'm good at and the gifts you've given me and use them to build up the church. Amen.

ponder

Don't just think about what you're good at; identify at least one strength in everyone you encounter today. Remember, we're all good at different things, so we shouldn't feel threatened by their strengths, we should celebrate them.

chat

Talk to a few people about what they're good at and what they're not good at. We're all good at some things and bad at others and that's OK. (That's not to say we shouldn't work on some of our weaknesses!) With this in mind, find out whether they're OK with not being good at some things and whether they are striving to improve.

write

If you have a photo of your church (the people, not the building), display it somewhere with the words of Romans 12:4,5 next to it.

action

If you search the internet you can find 'Spiritual Gift Questionnaires' that can help you identify your spiritual gifts. It can be obvious; however, many people find these questionnaires helpful. Chat to a church leader about this, and how you could best use your gifts to serve the church.

DAY 35: EVENING

For we are God's handiwork, created in Christ Jesus to do good works, which God prepared in advance for us to do.
Ephesians 2:10

pray
Creator God… thank you for the talents and gifts you have given me. Show me how I can use them to serve you and others. Remind me that the good work you've prepared for me to do is not just in the future, but in the present. Help me do everything as if I'm working for you. Amen.

ponder
Think about the fact that you are a unique creation of God, with a unique combination of skills, gifts, character traits and experiences, and each day you encounter unique situations. What opportunities does all of this provide you with to serve God in a way that no one else around you could?

TALK TOGETHER: DAYS 31–35

As individuals, what are our stories of approaching the cross of Christ and asking for forgiveness? What triggered our approach and what changed afterwards?

Day 31, 1 Peter 2:22–24

Why do we think that our lives are better with Jesus in them?

Day 32, 2 Corinthians 5:17,18,20

Where do we find it hardest to talk about the things of God? What makes these places and situations so difficult? How could we boost our confidence?

Day 33, Acts 1:4b,5,8

What perception do the people we know have of the church? How should we respond to this?

Day 34, Acts 2:42–47

What do we think each other's strengths are?

Day 35, Romans 12:4–8

DAY 36: MORNING

transformation

But the fruit of the Spirit is love, joy, peace, forbearance, kindness, goodness, faithfulness, gentleness and self-control. Against such things there is no law. Those who belong to Christ Jesus have crucified the flesh with its passions and desires. Since we live by the Spirit, let us keep in step with the Spirit. Galatians 5:22–25

When you sign up to be a Christ-follower, you sign up for a life of transformation. But don't forget, it's not primarily about transforming the lives of others or doing our little bit to change the world. First and foremost it's about being transformed ourselves; only when this happens are we able to be catalysts for the transformation of others and the world.

Transformation is not instant: it's a process. When we come to the cross, ask for forgiveness and put our faith in its power we are declared 'not guilty' and are reconciled to God. But it's difficult to leave our old life behind and embrace the new life. Old habits die hard and too often disobedience comes more naturally to us than obedience.

So, is transformation actually possible? Can a leopard change its spots? Jesus brings us hope; he believes that change is possible. He calls us to repent, to turn around, to leave our way of life behind, and begin living his way of life. Transformation is a long, and not always easy, walk. The key is to walk in step with the Holy Spirit. As you let the Spirit of God fill your life, the fruits of the Spirit will be the outward sign of your inward transformation.

pray

Gracious God… I want to repent. Help me leave my bad habits and unpleasant character traits behind and start walking in step with your Holy Spirit. Saturate my life with the Holy Spirit and grow within me love, joy, peace, patience, kindness, goodness, faithfulness, gentleness and self-control. Amen.

ponder

How can you grow more of the fruit of the Spirit in your life? (Maybe set an alarm to go off each hour, and after each alarm spend a few minutes thinking about one of the fruits.)

chat

Ask someone (perhaps your spouse, or close friend) to read through the fruit of the Spirit. Invite them to tell you which ones they think are obvious in your life and which need to be nurtured a little more!

write

Write each of the fruit of the Spirit on a separate, small, sticky label. Then attach these to nine pieces of fruit. Over the next few days, every time you eat a piece of fruit, think and pray about what you can do to nurture that fruit of the Spirit in your life.

action

Select one of the fruits that is not growing well in your life. Then, do a little research. For example, if you struggle with 'joy', ask a few people what a joyful life looks like, find the word 'joy' in a Bible concordance, or do some internet research on what it means to display 'joy-fruit' in your life. Then think and pray about how you are going to put this into action in your life.

I do not understand what I do. For what I want to do I do not do, but what I hate I do ... For I have the desire to do what is good, but I cannot carry it out. For I do not do the good I want to do, but the evil I do not want to do – this I keep on doing... What a wretched man I am! Who will rescue me from this body that is subject to death? Thanks be to God, who delivers me through Jesus Christ our Lord! Romans 7:15,18b,19,24,25

pray

My Saviour… there is no doubt that I am a sinner, saved only by your grace! Help me to do the good I plan to do and not the bad I don't plan to do. Make me increasingly alert to the promptings and guidance of your Holy Spirit. Amen.

ponder

What do you keep doing that you don't want to do? What don't you do that you want to do? What can you do to change this situation?

love one another

Love is patient, love is kind. It does not envy, it does not boast, it is not proud. It does not dishonour others, it is not self-seeking, it is not easily angered, it keeps no record of wrongs. Love does not delight in evil but rejoices with the truth. It always protects, always trusts, always hopes, always perseveres. Love never fails. 1 Corinthians 13:4–8a

This is one of the most well known passages in the Bible. It's the reading of choice at many, perhaps even most, church weddings. That's not surprising: the words are extremely poignant for marriage. However, when Paul wrote these words he wasn't thinking about love within marriage, he was talking about love within the church family, love amongst Christ-followers.

The early church brought together a great variety of people – Jews and Gentiles, rich and poor, men and women, slaves and slave-owners. Consequently, there was much conflict and disunity. Paul wanted love to be a distinguishing mark of Christian community. Without love the church couldn't present a loving God to the world, and it risked falling apart.

Fast-forward to today. How many times have you heard people talk about how they were attracted to the church community because they were blown away by the love that existed amongst it? Our love for one another attracts people to church and therefore can point people to Jesus. However, you probably know people who have walked away from church because they were fed up with Christians talking about love, but not loving one another. This hypocrisy, this lack of love, repelled them from church and away from Jesus. Love matters.

pray

Loving God… there are lots of different people in my church, and some of them I find a little difficult. Teach me how I can love them. May I be responsible for increased unity in the body of Christ, not the cause of any disunity. Amen.

ponder

Who, in your church, do you find difficult? While reflecting on the passage, pray for them, and ask God to focus your attention on their good points.

chat

Have a conversation with someone you know well and find out what causes them to find others difficult (for example, annoying habits, differing views). Then, go on to talk about how they try to cope with them. Also discuss what things they imagine people find difficult about themselves. Obviously, you should also answer the same questions for yourself!

write

Write the different attributes of love on some sticky notes. For example, 'Love is patient', 'Love does not boast' and 'Love always perseveres.' Then, stick them all around your home. (If you're married, you'll probably need to tell your spouse that you haven't put them up in order to drop hints at them!)

action

Make a loving gesture towards a person you find difficult in your church. For example, send them an encouraging email, apologise, invite them to a dinner party you're hosting, or offer to do something that will help them out.

DAY 37: EVENING

'A new command I give you: love one another. As I have loved you, so you must love one another. By this everyone will know that you are my disciples, if you love one another.'
John 13:34,35

pray
Son of God… when it comes to loving others – both the people I like and the people I dislike – help me follow in your example. I pray that our church will be well known for the love that exists within it, and the love we show for those who are outside it. Amen.

ponder
Do you know someone who has been put off church, Christianity and/or Jesus, because of a lack of love amongst or from Christians? What can you do to rectify the situation?

DAY 38: MORNING

points of connection

Paul then stood up in the meeting of the Areopagus and said: 'People of Athens! I see that in every way you are very religious. For as I walked around and looked carefully at your objects of worship, I even found an altar with this inscription: TO AN UNKNOWN GOD. So you are ignorant of the very thing you worship – and this is what I am going to proclaim to you.' Acts 17:22,23

As the good news of Jesus advanced into a pagan world, it must have felt that the message was so counter-cultural that it would never take root. I suspect that you often feel like that too.

The message of Jesus can sit uncomfortably with popular culture. Many of the values of Christianity are vastly different from the values of (post)modern Western society, and the (post) modern Western mind can struggle to get its head around many of our beliefs.

The example of Paul in Acts 17 is helpful. He doesn't begin by saying, 'People of Athens, your religion is a false religion.' Rather, his opening sentence seems like a compliment. We then discover that he had taken the time to learn about their religion and culture, and then he uses something from it as a springboard to talk about God. He finds a point of connection.

Many people today are dissatisfied with life, many are interested in the spiritual, there are a burgeoning number of movies exploring the supernatural and society is increasingly a multi-faith one. We are not short of points of connection, we just need to learn to spot them and then learn how to make the most of them.

pray

*Lord God… open my eyes and ears to what is going on around me.
Enable me to spot the points of connection and give me the courage
to use them as a springboard to introduce people to you and your
ways. Amen.*

ponder

In everything you do today be on the lookout for points of
connection. Don't just look in the obvious places like books,
newspapers and television!

chat

In your conversations today, if you spot a 'point of connection'
don't let it pass by. Seize the opportunity! Say a quick prayer,
and use the connection as a springboard. It could lead to some
fascinating God-flavoured conversations, which could point
people to the life-changing message of Jesus.

write

Write out the passage and place it somewhere that would
be a good source of 'points of connection' – for example, on
your television or magazine rack. Hopefully, when you see the
passage, you'll remember to be on the lookout!

action

Is there something that all your friends are talking about, yet you
know nothing about it? Perhaps a new TV series, book, movie
or advert. Who knows, it might be full of 'points of connection'!
Take some time to begin engaging with whatever they are
talking about. Start watching the TV series, borrow the book, or
take a trip to the cinema.

DAY 38: EVENING

Though I am free and belong to no one, I have made myself a slave to everyone, to win as many as possible. To the Jews I became like a Jew, to win the Jews ... To those not having the law I became like one not having the law ... so as to win those not having the law. To the weak I became weak, to win the weak. I have become all things to all people so that by all possible means I might save some.

1 Corinthians 9:19–22

pray

Heavenly Father… increase my eagerness for people to encounter Jesus and show me how best I can introduce my friends to him. Give me an abundant amount of wisdom to know how much I should become like other people, and in what ways I should be deliberately different. Amen.

ponder

Think of some of your friends. In what ways could you become more like them in order to introduce them to Jesus? (Eg taking an interest in their interests.)

DAY 39: MORNING

be prepared

Just as people are destined to die once, and after that to face judgment, so Christ was sacrificed once to take away the sins of many; and he will appear a second time, not to bear sin, but to bring salvation to those who are waiting for him. Hebrews 9:27,28

The Bible makes it clear that one day Jesus will return, defeat Satan once and for all, and judge everyone – those still alive, and those who have already died. However, it's not all that clear on exactly how this will all happen. Consequently, it is a subject of much debate and disagreement amongst Christians. Therefore, let us focus our attention on what's obvious, rather than what's more obscure.

You need to be ready for Christ's return or for your death, because you just don't know when you'll be standing before him as your judge. If you are a believer in Jesus, and have associated yourself with his death and resurrection, you do not have to be afraid. On the cross Jesus took your punishment, he has removed your sin and in return has given you the gift of his righteousness. Therefore, when you stand before Jesus his judgement will be 'not guilty'.

However, all this doesn't mean that you can spend the rest of your life doing whatever you want! The Bible reveals that you will have to give an account of your life and how you've used what God has given you. Your eternal life doesn't depend on this account, but the Bible places great importance on it, and suggests that we will be rewarded accordingly (1 Corinthians 3:13–15).

pray

Jesus, my judge and my saviour… thank you that I do not have to fear judgement. I pray that you will help me be a wise steward of all you have entrusted to me. Amen.

ponder

How does it make you feel that you don't have to live in fear of judgement? Do you think God will be pleased with the account of your life? If not, how could you be a better steward of what he has given you?

chat

Talk to someone about their experiences of waiting for judgement. For example, waiting outside the head teacher's office, or being pulled over by the police. If appropriate, find out what they think about the idea of God as judge. You might be quite surprised – many people like the idea that God will bring about justice.

write

Schedule an appointment (and set a corresponding alarm) for a randomly selected day, on your phone or computer. Title the appointment 'Christ's return', and if there is space, write out Hebrews 9:28b.

action

Set some time aside to consider whether you are making the most of your life and what God has given you. Begin by thinking about your money and time, your possessions and skills. And finally your relationships. For each area of your life, decide on one change you need to make.

... Why do you judge your brother or sister? Or why do you treat them with contempt? For we will all stand before God's judgment seat. It is written: '"As surely as I live," says the Lord, "Every knee will bow before me; every tongue will acknowledge God."' So then, each of us will give an account of ourselves to God. Therefore let us stop passing judgment on one another. Romans 14:10–13a

pray

Lord Jesus… whenever I am tempted to judge someone, remind me that you're the judge not me. Thank you that you are able to love and judge someone at the same time. Remind me that I'm not so good at that! Replace my judgemental thoughts with loving ones. Amen.

ponder
Have you had a judgemental attitude towards someone recently? Swap your judgemental thoughts for loving ones.

DAY 40: MORNING

hope for the future

Then I saw 'a new heaven and a new earth,' for the first heaven and the first earth had passed away, and there was no longer any sea ... I heard a loud voice from the throne saying, 'Look! God's dwelling-place is now among the people, and he will dwell with them. They will be his people, and God himself will be with them and be their God." He will wipe every tear from their eyes. There will be no more death" or mourning or crying or pain, for the old order of things has passed away.' He who was seated on the throne said, 'I am making everything new!' Revelation 21:1,3–5a

Do you like a happy ending? I have to confess, I think I prefer watching a movie with a happy ending rather than a realistic ending! The good news is it appears that our inbuilt desire for happy endings comes from our creator.

Without God stepping in it's hard to imagine a happy ending for planet Earth and its inhabitants. The earth's natural resources are distributed unfairly and used at a colossal rate; there's pollution, destruction, wars and natural disasters, not to mention our vulnerability in the vastness of space. A more realistic ending would surely be the annihilation of earth and its inhabitants.

But that's not God's plan! He assures us that for those who have been reconciled with him there is always hope for the future. After the final judgement God will be establishing a new heaven and a new earth – and it will be perfect. When tears are flowing we can look forward to a future with no tears. When we're in pain we can look forward to a future with no pain. Finally, God's will will be done on earth as it is in heaven.

pray

Creator God… thank you that you have a plan. When life is not going well, remind me of the hope I have for the future. May this future hope not lead to complacency but motivate me to act. Amen.

ponder

Do you live your life in the light of eternity and the future hope we have? How does the prospect of a hope-filled eternity bring perspective to your life?

chat

Talk to a few people today about their hopes and dreams for the future. Find out how their hopes and dreams affect how they approach their life in the present. If possible, chat to them about your beliefs concerning your long-term future and how this has a significant impact on your life in the present.

write

Do you remember how good it felt to be given a new exercise book at school? Perhaps you still get that feeling when you're starting a new notebook or diary? Next time you do, write some of Revelation 21:1,3–5a at the beginning of it, to remind you what the future holds.

action

As Christ-followers we're meant to be ambassadors of hope – to bring hope to those who have lost hope. Who do you know that is struggling at the moment? Perhaps someone who is crying, in pain or mourning? Do something to bring a little bit of hope into their life today.

When the perishable has been clothed with the imperishable, and the mortal with immortality, then the saying that is written will come true: 'Death has been swallowed up in victory' ... Therefore, my dear brothers and sisters, stand firm. Let nothing move you. Always give yourselves fully to the work of the Lord, because you know that your labour in the Lord is not in vain.

1 Corinthians 15:54,58

pray

Life-giving God… thank you that one day you'll exchange this temporary body of mine, with all its weaknesses, for a body that is everlasting. Thank you that you have the ultimate victory. Until that day, help me to stand firm. Amen.

ponder

As you go to sleep, do so with the words 'God will be victorious – good wins, evil is defeated' going around your head.

TALK TOGETHER: DAYS 36–40

Which fruit of the Spirit did each of us identify as one we struggle with? What are we all doing to nurture these weak fruits in our lives?

Day 36, Galatians 5:22–25

As a small group, or as a whole church, how can we become more loving towards one another?

Day 37, 1 Corinthians 13:4–8a

What are some of the points of connection we have identified this week? How can these be used as a springboard to talk about God?   173

Day 38, Acts 17:22,23

How does it make you feel that one day everyone who has ever lived will be judged? Why should knowing this make us less judgemental?

Day 39, Romans 14:10–13a

Do we live our lives in the light of eternity? How should the hope of eternity influence how we live our lives?

Day 40, Revelation 21:1,3–5a

KEEP READING...

It is my prayer that as you've made your way through this book over the past 40 days (or so!), your mind has become a healthier place, and consequently, you, and the people around you, have noticed a difference in your life. But what next? What are you going to do to ensure that your mind continues to become a healthy place?

Let me encourage you not only to keep reading the Bible every day, but to do so in a way that changes your mind and transforms your life.

For much of my life I've read a portion of the Bible every day. The problem was, once I'd done it, I crossed it off my to-do list and got on with the rest of my day. Rarely did reading the Bible make an impact on my life. More often than not, if someone had questioned me on the passage before I went to bed, I would have forgotten all about it!

There are a number of excellent Bible reading resources available – some are devotional in nature, while others are more study-based. I suggest you find one that works for you, and use it. However, in addition, I also suggest that you continue to practise some of the habits you've learnt while using 40/40. Don't just read the passage: ponder it throughout the day, talk to someone about it, write it down or do something that presents it in a symbolic way, and decide what one thing you are going to do in order to put what you've read into action.

Do not conform to the pattern of this world, but be transformed by the renewing of your mind. Then you will be able to test and approve what God's will is – his good, pleasing and perfect will. Romans 12:2

Closer to God is for anyone who longs to hear God's voice in today's noisy world. If you believe or hope that God speaks to ordinary people – loving, freeing, changing and healing them – then *Closer to God* is for you.

There's a Bible reading for every day of the week, but each weekly section is designed so that if you miss a couple of days you still won't get behind. There's lots to help with prayer, praise and reflection too.

£3.99

Daily Bread

A helpful, practical and inspiring guide that makes exploring the Bible enjoyable and relevant to everyday life.

£3.99

Encounter with God

A daily Bible guide designed for readers who want a thoughtful, in-depth approach to systematic Bible reading.

£3.99

Find more resources at www.WordLive.org